CANNABIS JOBS

CANNABIS JOBS

How to Make a Living and Have a Career in the World of Legalized Marijuana

ANDREW WARD

Skyhorse Publishing

Skyhorse Publishing books may be purchased in bulk at special discounts for sales promotion, corporate gifts, fund-raising, or educational purposes. Special editions can also be created to specifications. For details, contact the Special Sales Department, Skyhorse Publishing, 307 West 36th Street, 11th Floor, New York, NY 10018 or info@skyhorsepublishing.com.

Skyhorse® and Skyhorse Publishing® are registered trademarks of Skyhorse Publishing, Inc.®, a Delaware corporation.

Visit our website at www.skyhorsepublishing.com.

10 9 8 7 6 5 4 3 2 1

Library of Congress Cataloging-in-Publication Data is available on file.

Cover design by Qualcom
Cover photo credit:iStockPhoto.com

Print ISBN: 978-1-5107-4951-1
Ebook ISBN: 978-1-5107-4952-8

Printed in the United States of America

*To my family and friends who made this possible:
Mom, Dad, Hobbes, Grandmom, Jamie, Gab,
Oliver, and Delly in particular.*

Thanks to my detractors as well.

Table of Contents

Introduction   *ix*

Chapter 1: Medical   1

Chapter 2: Tech   11

Chapter 3: Cultivation   23

Chapter 4: Manufacturing, Production, and Processing   33

Chapter 5: Dispensaries   43

Chapter 6: Distribution and Delivery   55

Chapter 7: Testing   65

Chapter 8: Financial Services and Insurance   75

Chapter 9: Board Leaders and Executives   85

Chapter 10: Government, Law, Compliance, and Policy   97

Chapter 11: Creative PR, Branding, and Marketing   111

Chapter 12: Experiences, Events, and Entertainment   123

Chapter 13: Freelance   133

Chapter 14: Entrepreneur   145

Chapter 15: Maintaining Cannabis Culture   157

Acknowledgments   *169*

Introduction

The cannabis industry is booming and constantly evolving. So much so that some figures in this book could flip upside down by the time you are reading this. . In the United States and across the globe, a growing number of participants are entering the cannabis marketplace. Uruguay and Canada have legalized adult-use consumption, while 33 US states have some form of cannabis legislation as of August 2019. Additionally, countries in every continent have made some steps toward legalizing the plant.

January 2019 analysis of legal cannabis markets by BDS Analytics and The Arcview Group found that worldwide spending is expected to grow 39.1 percent in 2019, totaling $17 billion. This figure is attributed to the growth of the US market, as well as the number of adults consuming cannabis products.

In all, copious amounts of opportunities exist for job seekers and entrepreneurs alike. For some time, industry insiders knew that much of the world's job functions could be replicated in the cannabis space. Now, that possibility has come to fruition. Now it is expanding past these functions as the technology and needs of the industry increase.

While this book will delve extensively into the US markets, it would be a mistake not to recognize the emergence of foreign markets where cannabis interest and careers are also beginning to develop. *Marijuana Business Daily*'s "Countries to Watch" report delved into legalization around the world. It identified some countries where business opportunities are taking shape in legalized markets and others that may do so in the near future. They include:

- Australia
- Canada
- Chile
- Colombia
- Germany
- Israel
- Jamaica
- Lesotho
- Portugal

Our neighbor to the North is a particularly intriguing prospect. While Uruguay was the first country to legalize cannabis sales, it limited its offerings to citizens and through pharmacy sales. On the other hand, Canada's entrance into the cannabis market was for recreational consumption and sales purposes. Doing so was meant to provide access to citizens and stave off illicit market activity. However, its one-year ban on popular concentrates and edibles does pose a hurdle in achieving such goals.

Beginning sales on October 17, 2018, the country opened its marketplace to the masses. Professional consulting firm Deloitte's 2018 Canada Cannabis report expects legal sales to generate $4.34 billion in its first year of operations. With such a buzzing market, Deloitte expects Canada to reap the benefits of what some US states have begun to experience. The company explained in its report that, "What is certain is that legalization will open the doors to a dynamic, sophisticated industry that will create new jobs, new opportunities for businesses, and new revenues for government." The market should grow even more when edibles, vape cartridges, and topicals are legalized on October 18, 2019.

Opportunity could come soon enough for Mexico as well. While its laws can be complicated, judicial precedence has been set recently regarding key cannabis legislation. The key statute concerned the prohibition of recreational cannabis consumption. After the Mexican Supreme Court came to this decision on a fifth case, the ruling became precedence for the lower courts. Though the country's laws may halt the progress of the bill to some degree, investors from major companies abroad have made investments, including through mergers and acquisitions, in Mexico's cannabis companies.

Meanwhile, the United States continues to expand its cannabis access on the state level. Currently 11 allow for recreational, also known as adult use, consumption in the state. Meanwhile, an additional thirty-three allow for qualified patients to use cannabis as part of their treatment regimen.

With access growing, so has the industry. Businesses and career opportunities are popping up across the country thanks to a booming market. A report from Arcview Market Research and BDS Analytics projected that the legal American cannabis market could reach $23 billion in consumer spending by 2022. By that time, the market could produce more than 467,000 jobs.

That said, US job seekers do not have to wait until 2022 to see a career boom in the industry. A 2019 jobs report from Leafly found that the cannabis market currently provides 211,000 Americans with careers. These roles include all the types of producers, cultivators, processors, and others who work directly with the plant.

The report also noted the boom in cannabis careers occurring in indirect or ancillary jobs. In some circles, these roles are referred to as "not touching the plant" types of jobs and sectors. They, too, represent a significant boom in the industry.

Leafly reported, "When indirect and ancillary jobs—think of all the lawyers, accountants, security consultants, media companies, and marketing firms that service the cannabis industry—are added, along with induced jobs (local community jobs supported by the spending of cannabis industry paychecks), the total number of full-time American jobs that depend on legal cannabis rises to a whopping 296,000." In 2018, the industry added nearly 65,000 jobs in the US alone.

A January 2019 report by job search and review platform Glassdoor.com revealed staggeringly positive job figures across the board. Comparing listings on its own site, Glassdoor.com recorded 1,512 cannabis job postings in December 2018. The year prior saw only 857 cannabis career listings on the site—representing a 76 percent jump year-over-year.

Of the job listings recorded, 53 percent of the postings were for professional and technical workers. As the report's key findings note, "Market trends are driving increased demand for a wide variety of skills and backgrounds from marketing to plant sciences to accounting."

In fact, the number of jobs in professional and technical fields presents such diverse options that it pushes individual careers down on the list of most in-demand roles (according to the website). The analysis notes that the number of professional roles, including numerous managerial positions, should rise as the market legitimizes over time.

Concerning the frequency of listings, the website noted other professions which received an increased number of posts during its period of analysis. Service and retail jobs were prevalent, with brand ambassador and sales associate each comprising 5 percent of the listings. Other roles like store manager, wellness coordinator, and budtender received numerous listings on the site throughout this period. Physical labor roles including delivery and security work also appeared on the website's listings at a similar frequency.

Over the period, Glassdoor.com noted its top ten listed positions as brand ambassador, sales associate, store manager, wellness coordinator, delivery driver, general manager, assurance manager, lab technician, security guard, accountant, and budtender. None had more than 69 job postings during the period, with brand ambassador and sales associate having the most.

As evidenced by the above numbers, it is clear that additional growth is required. In addition to the numbers in individual fields proving to be rather small compared to developed industries, job locations lagged as well. While expected due to legal limitations, the cannabis careers listed on Glassdoor.com were clustered in most of the major markets. Some of the top cities listing on the website included San Francisco, Los Angeles, and Denver in the top three. New York City, which hadn't legalized adult-use marijuana as of May 30, 2019, was fourth on the list.

Overall, the analysis from Glassdoor.com concluded that the current demand emphasizes a need for professional and technical professionals. It cited three key reasons for the current demand. They centered on the market's push towards a legal, professional workforce that is capable of developing and growing tech-focused ventures.

Cannabis job recruiting platform Vangst's 2018 salary guide noted significant growth in the space as well. That includes a 690 percent increase in job listings between January 1, 2017, and August 1, 2018. An additional 220 percent growth was projected for 2019. The platform identified some of the hottest jobs in the space as Directors of Extraction or Cultivation and Compliance Manager, as well as roles in dispensaries, harvesting, and outside sales.

Data from both Glassdoor.com and Vangst revealed the potential for significant earnings in the space. The former used its "Know Your Worth" tool to determine that the median base cannabis industry salary was $58,511 annually. That is up from the US median salary of $52,943—a 10.7 percent drop in annual earnings. Yet, the report did note that the disparity of careers influenced the findings, with annual salaries ranging anywhere between $22,326 to $215,384 per year.

Vangst's data delved deeper into cannabis career salaries of its previously mentioned hottest jobs in the industry. While even a low skilled Director or Compliance Manager can earn a salary in the mid to upper $40,000 range, workers in dispensaries and cultivation can barely earn a minimum wage at the entry level. Conversely, a highly skilled Director or Compliance Manager can make close to or exceed $200,000 per year. Meanwhile, highly skilled dispensary and cultivation employees can still struggle to earn a livable wage, topping out at around $16 per hour in many markets.

The industry's adaptation to other market norms show signs of optimism in the job market. This is quite telling when it comes to employee benefits. Of those analyzed, Vangst found that 71 percent of respondents offered medical insurance to its employees. Additionally, 51 percent provided dental insurance and 46 percent did so for vision. Overall, 46 percent offered all three to its employees. And despite banking issues due to federal regulations, 29 percent reported offering 401k benefits to its workers.

The industry appears to be warming up for technical and professional workers, as well as entrepreneurs . . . although several factors could still make or break the industry and its impact on career potential. While many assume adult-use legalization is a matter of when, not if. Even so, regulations on several levels could still upend the process.

* * *

Federal regulations continue to loom over the heads of the industry. Cannabis was able to make it through the relatively brief stint that was rampant cannabis opponent Jeff Sessions's time as Attorney General. However, the industry knows that it is not out of the woods. While the next leading lawmakers appear less inclined to pursue states over their cannabis rights, the government's lies through the ages give anyone in the industry a rightful pause for concern.

Changes to federal law could alter the prospect mentioned

above. But nothing is certain, and any legalization forecasts should be taken with a grain of salt. That said, progress was made with the passing of the 2018 Farm Bill, which made hemp and CBD cultivation protected by federal regulations. While limits are still in place, cultivators in hemp-rich parts of the country (like Kentucky) now have more protections than ever before—hopefully allowing many to expand their operations and viability in the market.

Instead, legalization forecasts may be better applied on the state level. Numerous states began 2019 on the verge of passing adult-use cannabis regulations. Others have joined in as the year has gone on with little regressive measures being taken. Even in states where lawmakers are personally opposed to cannabis, such as Rhode Island and New Hampshire, officials understand that being surrounded by legal cannabis markets is not something they would like to have happen.

Local regulations can cause issues as well. Some states implemented stipulations where towns and counties can opt out of the program. In other cases, bans on certain types of products can limit business growth. Taxes have also proven to steer customers away from legalized shopping just as it drives businesses away due to high operating costs.

Most of America now appears to accept that cannabis will likely be legalized soon enough—by this book's publication. As such, countless individuals in the space are gathering their information and insights. While still a maturing industry rife with developing markets, these newcomers to the market do have source material to check their work against. This is occurring on the lawmaking and business planning aspects of the industry. When California and Colorado began the medical and recreational waves, it had no frame of reference. Today, new markets, entrepreneurs, and job seekers alike are able to learn from the high and low points of those markets and others—like Oregon and Washington—which have had some time to develop its marketplaces. The same can be said for Canada, as it completes its first year in operation on October 17, 2019.

With cannabis appearing to be on the cusp of legalization, markets are booming while others are developing. Each is searching for the talent to meet its growing demand. However, it is difficult, if not impossible, to find experienced cannabis workers due to a century of prohibition. As such, talented professionals from other sectors are being recruited to fill the void while scaling the industry.

This rapid hiring has left some proponents wondering if the industry is losing its ethos. While the outlaw days were okay to put away, the loss of an equal, communal spirit is not. Certainly, it was a foregone conclusion that the industry would change and normalize to a degree. However, many are not thrilled that passion is falling by the wayside while inclusive, diverse, and accessible efforts are not always at the top of a company or job seeker's priorities.

The opportunity presented by the cannabis industry appears to be once in a lifetime. For most (if not everyone) alive today, there has never been an industry of this magnitude in such demand for just about every type of profession and service to scale the industry. After over 100 or so years of being kept in the dark, cannabis is now the cash cow everyone wants to get their hands on.

For job seekers, this otherwise unheard-of opportunity is happening right now as this sentence is being read. Some roles and sectors are more in demand than others. It should be noted that, as innovation and access continue to expand, so too should the opportunities. To better understand this evolving market-place I spoke with professionals in numerous sectors to learn their needs and what lies ahead. We also discussed the highs (no pun intended) and lows of the industry and how they can be addressed today and beyond. And, most of all, they told me how you can start your own cannabis career.

That said, let's explore the cannabis market today and how you can be prepared to get involved.

1

Medical

Numerous sectors in the cannabis industry provide job seekers with multiple careers and pathways to finding a profession in the space. That is not the case when it comes to the medical sector. While it isn't just relegated to being a physician, the field is narrower than others. Much of the market is comprised of doctors who see patients and qualify them for cannabis ID cards. In this role, doctors can work part-time or make it a full-time feature of their work.

For many years, this meant seeing patients in an office. This left medical professionals able to only serve patients who could get access to their offices. Now, advancements in technology allow practitioners and patients to connect much easier. In several states, prospective patients can now meet with a physician online. Commonly known as telemedicine, practitioners continue to evaluate patients as they normally would, except now done through a third-party. Doctors become affiliated with the company and see patients through the third-party company's online portal. In most cases, the pay seems to vary between $60 and $200 per hour.

Ryan Lepore, Business Operations Manager at PrestoDoctor, a telemedicine service in New York, California, and Nevada, explained to me the benefits of telemedicine. These benefits extend to patients and the sector at large. "Telemedicine has been a natural ally for medicinal cannabis patients, allowing many to privately address their health concerns in an already stigmatized patient experience. Within their own convenience, patients are afforded access to a cannabis-specific physician regardless of a clinic's proximity, and provided lower expenditures for a medical experience that currently does not allow for insurance co-pays. Many online telemedicine clinics have been able to service larger population demands in select states, conjointly, providing reliable entry points for medical data and academic research through already digitized patient files."

Meanwhile, Dr. Harry McIlroy noted the range can vary a bit more, between $80 and $500. "Some practitioners also charge more for ongoing care. This can range from $600–$1000 per year for routine follow-up to make corrections."

While in-person and telemedicine doctors make up the majority of the sector, they are not the only career path in the medical field. In some cases, medical professionals can serve as liaisons for companies and research facilities. Often, a liaison's central role is to be an educator, discussing the plant and the human body among other topics. Additionally, a person in this role may be the face of a brand or institution while also meeting with patients for consultations. In some other cases, they may build relationships with local physicians to establish a peer-to-peer network in the community.

Support roles are vital to the work. For example, a patient care coordinator may be tasked with assisting patients and families to determine treatment courses while helping doctors maintain a functioning practice. This sort of work will earn a more modest salary of around $15 per hour.

Experienced medical professionals can also enter the cannabis space—and not just in their office. The insights and wisdom medical professionals possess is needed in the boardroom making executive decisions. Cannabis producers and distributors often bring on medical professionals to oversee areas such as medical research and development. Depending on the specialty of the doctor, their focus could delve into areas including pain management, strain specificity, and much more.

Niche sectors of the market are opening as physicians and patients alike allow medical cannabis into the equation. One such area is physical therapy. In recent years, the community has made efforts to educate physical therapists and physical therapist assistants about the pros and cons of cannabis use and PT.

In a 2018 article for the American Physical Therapy Association's website, Johanns Gammel, PTA, explained how medical marijuana helped ease a patient's multiple sclerosis (MS) pains and improve their PT. After using marijuana, "sometimes, the spasms, twitches, and pain subside within one minute,"

Gammel says. "This allows me to stretch his legs, which are tight from the disease and from his being in a wheelchair. The effects of MMJ help him get the proper manual therapy in accordance with the PT's plan of care in order to be able to move."

The adverse effects of cannabis on some created another niche need in the market: rehabilitation. While some refute the notion marijuana is indeed addictive to some though most estimate that this number is less than 10 percent of users. Though much of the market won't experience this outcome, for those that do, rehab could be the best thing to get them back on track. Those specializing in this field may become familiar in cognitive-behavioral, contingency management, and/or motivational enhancement therapy to help treat a patient.

CBD is fast becoming its own field in cannabis, with a particular interest in its possible medical applications. Dr. Hervé Damas is the founder of Grassroots Medicine and Wellness in Florida. While he didn't say CBD would become its own field of medical services, he does see its potential. "I believe the CBD segment will be the largest segment in the cannabis industry in ten years," Dr. Damas predicted. In addition to CBD, Dr. Damas sees prescribing physicians remaining as an in-demand role. As will treatment experts.

Me Fuimaono-Poe, a Family Nurse Practitioner at The Malie Cannabis Clinic in Hawaii, hopes to see a demand for additional research in the years to come. "Berkeley just announced a cannabis research program and we are so excited," said Fuimaono-Poe. While thrilled over the news, she noted other areas more specific to the sector that are more in demand. She mentioned the need for cannabis clinicians who are willing to do certifications and provide dosing guidelines. "Having people get their advice from a twenty-year-old budtender is not going to cut it anymore."

Unlike other sectors, the medical field rightly has some hard and fast rules that one must adhere to. Namely, they need the proper education and certification to even attempt entering the sector. In a 2018 article for the online social networking service for medical professionals Doximity, Dr. Rachna Patel, explained how she became a cannabis doctor. She chose the field because she wanted to make a meaningful change in people's lives. Working in a traditional practice led her to a realization. "While going through training in Emergency Medicine, I was handing out prescriptions, on the one hand. But, on the other hand, I found myself treating the side effects of these prescription medications. I encountered patients that had become addicted to these prescription medications. And, I was in the unfortunate position of resuscitating patients that had overdosed on these prescription medications."

For the next year, Dr. Patel studied marijuana and began her journey to becoming a medical cannabis expert. She told Doximity how she took her first steps in the field and how it impacted her. "After spending a year digging through the research on medical marijuana, I saw its potential as a much safer alternative to prescription medications. In fact, when I signed up to work at a medical marijuana clinic, I was taken aback by the clinical outcomes I saw. Many of my patients, with the use of medical marijuana, were able to eliminate the use of their prescription medications altogether!"

In addition to reading up on the subject and working in the field. Dr. McIlroy suggested joining groups like the Society of Cannabis Clinicians and watching webinars to immerse yourself further in the sector and its developments.

Meanwhile, Bryan Passman, founder of cannabis industry search firms The GIGG (for staffing) and Hunter + Esquire, explained the difficulty of getting into the sector. "At this point, you have to fight and claw your way into it. We work with physicians who have carved out time in their very busy schedules and money out of their personal budgets to hire copyrights to publish papers that will attract industry attention, as well as to do all that they can to win speaking engagements at relevant industry trade shows." He went on to note the importance of passion. "You don't have to be a cannabis doctor or nurse, but you do have to be passionate about your pursuit of entry and be willing to pay a price up front to separate yourself from the pack of candidates, but that really goes for all executive roles."

Due to a lack of federal regulations, each state has its own set of rules to becoming a registered cannabis physician. Therefore, there is no uniform system one can follow to becoming a doctor in the marijuana space. Instead, they must check the rules and regulations in their state and adhere to them as such. Some states will be more complicated than others.

Aside from finding a career, job seekers should know about some of the most discussed topics in the space. A good deal of discussion is likely to center on local and state regulations. This is especially true in states where its medical markets are just coming to fruition.

From there, many topics stretch beyond state borders and impact the sector as a whole. One of the more looming and concerning issues is the continued information gap between patients and physicians. In far too many instances, patients know more about cannabis than their medical professional. This isn't a "vaccinations cause autism" sort of blind distrust in physicians, either. In this case, many physicians are reluctant to learn about, much less recommend, cannabis to their patients.

In short, the reluctance is due to two justified, yet frustrating reasons. First, medical cannabis does not fit the mold of traditional, modern remedies and requires much more variation than other medication. Second, many doctors do not want to bother with cannabis due to the often limited clinical studies and its legal status. The latter holding up progress on the former in the United States.

Influential medical groups continue to dissuade physicians from participating as well. In a November 2018 article, Tony Leys of the *Des Moines Register* noted how the Iowa Medical Society considers the state's medical cannabis program an "unsustainable and dangerous public policy." Leys reported that the group has even told doctors that they could experience legal and insurance issues if they participate in the marketplace.

As such, a growing number of patients want to explore marijuana for medical treatment, but must discuss the matter with a professional who has no understanding of the plant.

In addition to an education gap affecting many, two significant groups of the American public, seniors and veterans, feel left out of the medical market. This includes a late winter 2019 decision by the Missouri Veterans Commission that ruled its residents in numerous nursing homes could not take part in the state's medical cannabis program.

Meanwhile, making matters more troubling and frustrating, other states must contend with an influx of dubious offices and practitioners who could upend the market. Debbie Knight told the *Tampa Bay Times* that when she went into the offices of her closest and most affordable cannabis doctor, Fort Lauderdale 420 Marijuana Doctors, she had a terrible experience. She reported a foul smell, discarded fast food bags in the exam room, and misleading prices that differed from what she read online. After her visit, Knight never received her license and could not reach the office further, as its phone was disconnected two weeks later. In addition to dodgy doctors and groups causing fear and information gaps, the market is shifting away from its roots, explained Fuimaono-Poe. "Basically, the change from this is medicine to this is alcohol-like, 'Let's tax the fuck out of [cannabis] and get rich' model has created a marketplace that isn't geared towards compassionate use." She elaborated, "The change from high-quality cannabis to crappy cannabis grown in football-sized domes under lights has impacted our markets in ways we don't fully understand yet."

Despite the series of pressing concerns, the industry does offer scores of positives as well. While Dr. Damas did note regulatory ambiguity and the stigma attached to cannabis, he saw immense good from the sector. He stated the grassroots movement of the community and its "well-intentioned people."

Meanwhile, Fuimaono-Poe noted a decrease in stigma over her years in the business. Though the influx of misinformed newcomers does not sit well with the industry veteran. "The story I am most sick of hearing is, 'I didn't even use cannabis until two years ago. Then, I tried it, and now I own two dispensaries and a grow . . . '"

When finding ideal applicants, Dr. Damas looks outside the box. A former NFL player for the Buffalo Bills, Dr. Damas values experience that goes beyond the plant. "[I value] experience outside of the cannabis industry, self-discipline, an independent worker." Meanwhile, Fuimaono-Poe singles out flexibility as an ideal trait. "This is a rapidly growing and evolving market. If you don't have resiliency, you will hate it here."

When looking back at their own experiences, both have had enjoyable experiences overall. "I give people hope and I provide answers to questions that were going unanswered," remarked Dr. Damas. He is particularly hopeful of the gains he could provide to his specialty. "With my research, I'm doing work that will hopefully have a permanent impression on the landscape of sports and medicine."

For Fuimaono-Poe, she considers her cannabis experience a beautiful time. "I have come to learn that this is not a simple plant. It's more of a complex entity," she noted, adding, "I have seen it completely change people's lives." She briefly elaborated on some of her rewarding work. "I have aided several patients in successfully titrating off all opiates and benzodiazepines using cannabis. Cannabis provides profound healing on really deep levels."

2

Tech

The technology boom has steadily grown over the past several decades. That is true for cannabis as well. While hamstrung by the law, the illicit market continued to innovate cannabis products for years while skirting the law. For example, with extraction technology, first came dangerous home extraction methods using butane and tubes during the illicit market days. Then came hair straighteners, a process that eliminated solvents but provided little consistency to product yields. Now, with state-of-the-art facilities, these extraction methods and others provide consumers with legal products they can pick up in plenty of states.

This technology has spilled into the mainstream as more regions pass cannabis legislation. With regulated markets, cannabis technology has flourished in short order. Yet, still, scores of items have not yet hit the market—meaning there are still ample opportunities for entrepreneurs and job seekers alike in the space.

With demand already there, job seekers do not need to wait to get involved in the sector. That said, the issues surrounding some states hinder labs and future opportunities.

David Hua is the founder and CEO of Meadow, a cannabis dispensary point-of-sale software company. Hua explained how the cannabis industry as a whole has been underserved with technology. Due to prohibition, most cannabis ventures couldn't have access to world-class technology solutions. "The result was a patchwork of various pieces of technology to help get their jobs done," Hua explained.

Lulu Tsui, tech entrepreneur and co-founder of REVEL, expanded on the sector's shortcomings in today's cannabis market. "The first required seed-to-sale tracking software offerings were legacy systems used in other industries and then hacked together to try and serve the cannabis. My background is in user experience, so I think that the majority of software tools for the cannabis industry is still being designed in an antiquated way—most are still designing around the system instead of designing for the user. Just ask any operator how they feel about the software in their facility."

Now, as legalization expands, Hua notes that unprecedented growth is currently underway in the industry, and is fueled by capital. As such, numerous sectors are reaping the benefits.

When asked about booming cannabis tech sectors, Eric

Vlosky, the marketing director for rosin extraction technology producer PurePressure, said that opportunity is everywhere. He said, "Put it another way, which areas aren't booming?

"Processing is the future of cannabis, and many people understand this keenly. In every case so far, as markets mature, the demand for processed and concentrated products grows enormously. This trend will only continue to increase innovation in extraction into hyperdrive."

"With respect to technology, we're seeing growth in all parts of the supply chain," Hua pointed out, while also expanding on the growth across the industry. "At cultivation, we're seeing automated greenhouses, tissue culture for clones, machinery to help with sorting, and packaging of flower. At the manufacturing level, we're seeing an evolution of cannabinoid extraction technology resulting in many more form factors of extracts suitable for a spectrum of consumption methods. At the distribution level, we're seeing best practices from other industries to help with logistics and inventory management. At the dispensary level, we're seeing companies like Meadow build custom tools for the operators and their customers with a seasoned technology team with backgrounds in design, security, and scalability."

Shanel Lindsay is the founder and president of the decarboxylation tech brand Ardent Cannabis. Decarboxylation, in its simplest form, is the process which converts the non-intoxicating cannabinoid THCA into THC so consumers can feel the effects of cannabis. Like Hua, she is excited about the growth and developments in the space. She believes that home testing is the next frontier in cannabis tech. "Lab testing is fantastic, but your average person does not have access to a lab," she explained. Between some home growers and the illegal market, it is important to understand what is in a plant. As such, Lindsay sees a huge gap in the space today. "There's a huge desire for people to be able to quantify and know what is in whatever product that they've been growing." She also pointed out that an option is not currently available.

Unlike some other sectors, cannabis tech does offer some insights into its pay range. Hua suggested visiting AngelList for some insights into tech jobs. Meanwhile, data from ZipRecruiter.com shows a varying range of pay for its these jobs. They range from front-end software development internships to leaders in the space. Modest to average livable salaries are available to Chemistry Analysts, who can earn $40,000 to $50,000. Extraction and distillation tech work can net a person between $30,000 and $60,000 annually. Higher up the ladder, we find that presidents of engineering can earn well into the six figures, with one position topping out at $250,000 annually.

Looking at tech in general, global HR consulting firm Robert Half's 2019 analysis of tech salaries found that 43 percent of industry leaders are willing to increase wages and compensation packages when they hire for certain positions.

Its breakdown of tech salaries found that a highly skilled CIO (Chief Information Officer) or CTO (Chief Technology Officer) can earn well above $250,000. Meanwhile, even most other positions down the ladder pay newcomers a livable salary for most regions of the country. A few exceptions, such as lower skilled help desk team members, certain technicians, and computer operators may struggle with wages often starting at under $40,000 per year.

On Indeed.com, some technician careers are listed. Most salaries ranged from $12 to $20 an hour depending on the work and location. Additional technician roles listed on the site mentioned annual salaries that could reach upwards of $70,000.

Speaking of location, Robert Half showed that starting tech salaries vary on a number of factors. As such, a tech salary in Chicago and New York City will be a significant percentage above the national average. This includes smaller cities like Paramus, New Jersey, and Tyson Corners, Virginia. Meanwhile, areas like Duluth, Minnesota, and Kalamazoo, Michigan, could see significantly lower starting salaries compared to the average.

With such a wide diverse set of needs across the industry, job seekers can enter with a variety of skills and backgrounds. Eric Vlosky remarked how just about anyone from any background can make an impact in cannabis, singling out some key areas. "Of course, agricultural or pharmaceutical specialties are particularly demanded, but also supply chain experts, interior retail design, software, and more are all being drawn to the flame."

At Meadow, Hua's team comprises of engineers and software developers in addition to sales, business development, and marketing professionals. "We've seen that people with backgrounds in alcohol and pharmaceuticals are particularly well equipped to understand the limitations around marketing a product that is so heavily regulated." That said, the company keeps an open mind to job seekers, "But really, anyone with an entrepreneurial spirit and a desire to roll up their sleeves and learn a new industry could make great additions to the market."

As such, certain roles do require college degrees. A technician is almost sure to need a bachelor's degree while a web developer may be able to be certified through alternate learning courses or even learn on the job. Be sure to look into your field or fields of interest and determine what education and professional background is needed.

Meanwhile, Robert Half's tech salary report noted that project professionals are in high demand—as are hybrid job skills that sit between IT and other departments like marketing or operations.

The report noted some of the top tech certifications in demand at the moment. They are:

- Agile and scrum
- AWS Certified Solutions Architect Certified Ethical Hacker (CEH)
- Certified Information Systems Security Professional (CISSP)
- Cisco Certified Network Associate (CCNA)
- Cisco Certified Network Professional (CCNP)
- CompTIA A+
- Global Information Assurance Certification (GIAC)
- IT Infrastructure Library (ITIL)
- IT Service Management (ITSM)
- Microsoft Certified Solutions Expert (MCSE)
- MCSE: Cloud Platform and Infrastructure
- Project Management Professional (PMP)

Additionally, the report listed the in-demand technical skills sought across most industries. They are:

- .NET
- Angular
- Apache Spark
- Artificial intelligence (AI)
- Augmented reality (AR)
- Blockchain
- C#
- Cloud and SaaS

- Golang
- Hadoop
- Java
- JavaScript
- Machine learning (ML)
- Microsoft SQL Server
- PHP
- Python
- R
- ReactJS and React Native
- Ruby on Rails
- SAS
- Swift
- Virtual reality (VR)
- Virtualization (Amazon web services, Microsoft Hyper-V, and VMware)

Those working in the sector reported enjoying the new challenges, growth potential, and possible payday a rapidly evolving landscape has to offer. As such, cannabis tech is often regarded as an exciting space, even more than many of the emerging spaces in the marketplace.

The need for innovation, development, and funding has led to a surge of networking communities across the country. In New York City alone, bustling cannabis networking communities like High NY, REVEL, and CannaGather meet monthly or quarterly to discuss pressing subjects in the space. Topics include regulations, obtaining capital, and criminal justice reform. There, established professionals, job seekers, and enthusiasts alike can meet and learn. Those seeking to make lasting introductions may find success at such gatherings.

Other topics discussed include expansion outside of the market—a new step for cannabis. Instead of having brands branch into the space, CannaRegs, a cannabis legal data platform, announced in February 2019 that its parent company, Regs Technology, closed a $2 million funding round for outside growth. The money raised is slated to go toward growing outside of the industry to provide legal technology for other highly regulated spaces.

Meanwhile, the industry continues to discuss innovation coming from outside the United States. This includes regular tech breakthroughs in Israel and Canada. Other countries are getting in on the mix as well. The island nation of Malta is one unlikely medical cannabis tech competitor with a recent track record for tech innovation. In recent years, the country embraced both blockchain and AI. In 2019, Malta's Prime Minister, Dr. Joseph Muscat, went on record as saying his country will allow medical marijuana while also exporting to the global market. Plus, the Malta Cannabiz Summit hopes to put a stamp on its cannabis events much like Spannabis does in Spain.

That said, it takes a particular business structure and team members to be successful. As Hua laid out, "it requires nimble teams to build flexible solutions that can scale with the growth of the industry." Thankfully, many note the cannabis community spirit is very much alive in the sector. As Vlosky noted, "people are friendly and passionate about it so there is a lot of comradery." This does not mean other personalities aren't entering the market. Vlosky was quick to regard that the industry does have its fair share of "hyper-egotistical" people in the sector.

Another drawback Vlosky noted was a lack of diversity in tech and cannabis altogether. "Generally speaking, the cannabis space is a heavily male-dominated industry at both the ground level and at the top." He added that "Many industries are this way, so that fact by itself doesn't mean it's purposefully exclusive, but my hope is that as many people as possible from different backgrounds and ethnicities will actively join the industry."

The sector has some misconceptions to contend with as well. Vlosky noted that they include the emergence of the industry, as well as its tech. "In reality, the illicit market and the tireless work of NORML, plus other innumerable industry advocates were instrumental getting the cannabis out of the darkness and into true legal territory." Thanks to these efforts, many innovations that have been in the shadows are now becoming multi-million and billion-dollar products, and services for the market.

These products and services create solutions for the cannabis industry. As Hua mentioned, such answers and innovations come from within cannabis as well as outside industries that are being layered, of sorts, into the cannabis space. "Cannabis is really nuanced," he said, "from the chemistry of the product to the regulatory requirements. It's important to understand how these various solutions solve these specific needs that other industries may not have addressed."

When it comes to the people needed to provide these solutions and services, Hua explained how an ideal candidate is able to work in an industry that has never existed before. "An ideal applicant is someone who thrives in uncertainty and is able to make logical decisions while dreaming big and maintaining a can-do attitude."

A standard answer across the industry about ideal personality traits is passion. Vlosky believes this passion is essential for these job seekers. He said a high-quality job seeker in cannabis is "someone who is passionate about cannabis and believes in its

ability to do good for the world, whether it's medicinal or adult
use to help people feel the way they want to feel, safely. Passion
is the bedrock of drive in this industry."

When I spoke to Ardent's CEO Lindsay, she emphasized the
need for having a specific set of skills. That particular set of skills
won't cut it alone, though. She explained how an independent
worker is in demand for a number of rapidly growing companies. "We're really, really busy," she remarked. "Being able to
come on and independently contribute based on the knowledge
you developed in your skillset" is an intangible ideal for Ardent
and many other companies in the sector. The value of this trait
can help an employee transcend such a title. "It's almost like the
thought process of a partner rather than an employee."

Lindsay's sentiment represents the feelings of the massive sector. One day the market may become more of a teaching industry. But with so much work and time to be made up in short
order, teaching takes a back seat to innovation and scalability.
Lindsay expanded on her thought: "That strong ability to take
charge and lead, while also understanding and knowing how to
be patient and work within the current system, I think kind of
describes the ideal personality."

With a few years of experience under their belts, respondents
have understood that the cannabis tech sector is just like the
marijuana industry altogether: It is still wild and evolving. Or,
as Vlosky put it, "It wouldn't be a stretch to say [cannabis is] the
fastest evolving industry in the world. From regulatory hurdles
to cannabis-specific technologies, it's a chaotic space that favors
the agile."

Looking toward the future, Vlosky projects for a good deal of
processing, scaling, and intense competition. "As demand grows
for new product experiences, so will the need to process cannabis

into all manners of different things." With that increased demand, he projects an uptick in efficiency. "To fulfill that soon-to-be global demand, everything is also in the process of scaling up for greater efficiency." He also noted that the green rush will ramp into a new gear once the US changes cannabis on a federal level.

"Overall, I am proud to be a part of the industry and I love every second of the chaos."

3

Cultivation

Cannabis cultivation is a sector of the industry that remains largely influx. Unlike many spaces, the opportunity to thrive in the sector appears to be somewhat limited. Due to regulations, the both the illicit market and legal markets continue to struggle with a series of pain points. Also thanks to laws, the mainstream market struggles with a series of pain points. As such, all sides of the market suffer as the rest of the supply chain is affected by the mess that has become much of the market. Conversely, growers in some parts of the country report doing well and see promise for the future.

The answer is less clear-cut at this time. Cannabis cultivation careers vary by state. Without a lack of federal regulations, each state must make its own rules. What came from them varies wildly, which is why many claim the sector is not one for job seekers at this time.

As *Marijuana Business Daily*'s 2018 Cultivation Snapshot summarized, "Those like Oregon with long-entrenched illicit markets and plentiful outdoor farms suffer from oversupply, driving prices down. Contrast that with relatively new programs, such as Nevada and Alaska, which are reporting strong wholesale markets—for the time being." It added, "Then there's California, which is its own ever-changing, massively complicated behemoth."

The report went on to note that wholesale cannabis is plunging as well. Down from the year prior's $1,600 per pound, 2018 found pounds selling at $1,300. "As more businesses are licensed and cultivators build out their facilities and become more efficient, this trend line is likely to continue on the same downward trajectory," the report explained.

In the end, the promise of a better cultivation day may not come from THC, but rather CBD. Thanks to changes in federal regulation, hemp has entered back into the mainstream. Giving hope to a number of cultivators, hemp could be the cash crop that pulls many out of a sagging profession. This is especially true for cultivators in Colorado, Kentucky, and Montana, some of the top hemp cultivation states in the US. While it still remains mired in regulations, the progress made in the 2018 Farm Bill has the industry and its cultivators buzzing.

With such movement in the industry over the past few years, it seems as if the entire cultivation landscape has been upended. What was once a booming outlaw culture situated in locations like Mendocino and Humboldt Counties in California are now mainstream. Outdoor grows are replaced by large-scale, mostly indoor facilities that churn out product for the legal market.

When I spoke with "Terry," a long-time cannabis operator on both sides of the market, they explained to me how there is no opportunity left to become a illicit-market grower. Even the few chances remaining for employment on the illicit market are fading away due to the marketplace. "There will always be room for trimmers but, at this point, there are industrial alternatives. Because the price per raw pound of top-shelf biomass of indoor/outdoor has dropped so dramatically, it doesn't mean you can't pay a trimmer $150, $200 a pound. It's $100." To keep pace with production costs, many of Terry's colleagues have turned to illegal labor.

Terry went on to explain how the shift happened just as recently as a three to four years ago. At that time, a large chunk of the industry was supported by small-scale, post-hobbyist grows. Such grows would cultivate in houses, multiple garages, small warehouses, and other such locations. With a price collapse two years ago, everything changed. The situation only heightened as the legal market began to be consolidated—so much so that the number of pounds that are produced per year in California have increased. At the same time, the number of growers producing have decreased.

"Where traditionally growing was an accessible point in the legal marketplace, it no longer is . . . I know professional master growers in Oregon who are making $60,000 a year."

On the legal market, the cultivation sector varies by state. For example, in 2018, Colorado's robust industry with indoor and outdoor growers dominated in different parts of the state. Demand was strong and led to more entering the market. The rise in registrations led some to call for a pause of licensing additional growers to stave off falling prices. Prices were expected to decline as vertically integrated operations stood to benefit the most.

Anthony Franciosi, the founder of Colorado's Honest Marijuana Company, utilizes all-natural cultivation methods to create his products. He noted that state laws can be daunting to young companies. "In Colorado, the industry is extremely regulated, and compliance can be the straw that breaks a young company's back if fines or license suspensions take place." He noted that those looking to break into the sector may want to consider entry-level work as a trimmer or budtender. Also, applicants should note that jobs don't always last in the industry. "There is an extremely high turnover rate throughout the industry. So, if you find a solid place to work and put your time in, there is definitely opportunity to be had."

The market is not entirely bleak or short-lived. There are roles in the cultivation space. Aside from the previously mentioned positions, job seekers with applicable experience could skip the entry-level and find work as an assistant grower or technician, where they'll assist master growers. In addition to growing, management positions are needed. They include facilities manager, who tends to the needs of the grow. Meanwhile, a production manager relies often on business savvy employees to ensure that everything is running smoothly.

Unfortunately, the salaries for these positions are not nearly as lucrative as other sectors offer. Roles listed on Indeed.com in the winter of 2019 approximately averaged around $15 per hour, with annual wages reaching between $40,000 and $50,000. On the other hand, in the summer of 2018, Cannabis At Work, a Canadian job connection community, found that there was a high demand for skilled cultivators. That said, this was applicable only to Canada.

The path to a cultivation career is not limited to just one or two ways. A job seeker can follow the path of Craig Zaffe, the founder of Long Island, New York's Your CBD Oils. Zaffe is a life-long horticulturalist and cannabis consumer. Over the years, he became enamored with CBD and its ability to become an asset to the community. Now, to stay in touch with the community and grow his business, Zaffe is an active vendor and visitor at many of New York's networking events and parties.

You could also follow a path similar to Franciosi, who moved out to Colorado from New Jersey at age eighteen. Working seasonal jobs and snowboarding, he got involved in more than just cannabis consumption. "A couple of the guys I landscaped with had been growing for a long time and showed me how they were doing it, which was always all-natural in the soil. So, I have always been trying to grow all-naturally. After a number of years like that, I was able to meet some amazing people who believed in the craft cannabis mentality and wanted to be in the business, and we formed Honest MJ to try and deliver the cleanest marijuana products around."

* * *

Those needing to learn more before entering the space may want to go out to the Bay Area and get educated on horticulture at Oaksterdam University, the leading name in cannabis industry education. Classes are held each semester, and in accelerated courses. In addition to Oaksterdam, some colleges and universities have begun to offer classes on the field, with more likely to be offered as the demand grows. Be sure to stay up to date on courses being offered locally at universities, community colleges, and other educational events. Between online and the rising offerings in many local markers, the accessibility to a cannabis education is only expected to get easier as time goes on.

It would be wise to brush up on the current events in the sector as well. Of all the news, the 2018 Farm Bill has to be the biggest in the sector, if not the entire industry. The long, drawn-out process concluded with President Trump signing the bill into law at the end of 2018. The Farm Bill did plenty for the farming industry. Overall, it legalized hemp, providing the coverage and opportunity cultivators needed and deserved.

Under the new regulations, states and tribal governments can set their own laws as well. Additionally, cultivators face significantly less risk of running into the law. Even more, their hemp crops finally qualify for federal crop insurance. As such, the industry is much more legitimized while finally receiving the protections other crops have in the US.

While THC cultivation may offer little opportunity, hemp cultivation may present opportunities on the legal market. This has been the case in Oregon over the past year. After its cultivation market became flooded with product, its cultivators scrambled to make up for the plummeting cost of flower. Instead of shying away from cannabis, some have shifted gears toward hemp. Outdoor growers saw an opportunity to pivot and diversify their harvests slightly. The state's hemp market has fewer restrictions than cannabis, including allowing for much more land used for farming. Plus, hemp cultivation prices are lower, easing the income burden Oregon currently faces.

To keep marijuana cultivators in the mix, the state considered a bold step in early 2019. To combat its overstock issues, some lawmakers wanted to allow for the export of Oregon's cannabis to other states. The proposal got people buzzing but, in the end, won't amount to anything until the law changes on the federal level. Regardless, the proposal could significantly help the industry. For example, in Illinois, the potential for legalization has many wondering if the state's cultivators could grow enough to meet demand. If allowed, Oregon's excess could keep states like Illinois free of such worries. Oregon continued to advance the issue into the spring of 2019.

With little options to succeed in THC, numerous state farmers have gone back to the illicit market. Many have falsely listed their crops as destroyed on the state registry and begun moving it through intermediaries and selling out of state. When faced with the prospect of burning thousands of dollars of product or selling across state lines, it isn't surprising which option plenty are choosing.

Outside of Oregon, there appears to be little to any promise for the sector. Kris Krane, President of 4 Front Ventures, wrote in a 2018 *Forbes* post that investing in a grow operation now would be historically unwise. "Investing in large-scale cannabis cultivation today is like playing the end of alcohol prohibition by buying a hop farm." Instead, Krane suggested where an investment would be better spent. "What investors should be more focused on is controlling brands and the distribution points for those brands."

With the sector rapidly being absorbed by mega-money

players, as well as vertical integration laws in many states, Krane's estimation appears accurate. For Honest Marijuana's Franciosi, he enjoys being at the forefront of a burgeoning industry. Though there is concern that further intrusion by large brands could harm the reputation of the product. He explained how he feels that the market's consolidation has led to a decline in the crop. Krane believes that this has led to craft producers being driven out by products that are lower in price and quality but have superb marketing efforts.

Even so, the negatives do not stop many cannabis cultivators from continuing to grow for a living. On both sides of the market, the need is dwindling as big money and regulations enter the picture. Yet there is belief that hemp can provide lifeblood to the sector and cannabis overall.

For Franciosi, he's looking for people in it for more than a short while. "I like to find people who are committed to living in the area." In addition to loving Colorado, he prefers someone who isn't looking to jump to another sector. "They aren't necessarily looking for their next big opportunity in the cannabis industry, but a chance to be part of a community and a team."

That said, job seekers should be prepared for the reality of the industry. Opportunities will be available, but at lower frequencies than other fields. The pay is likely to be less as well. That said, the passion of cannabis cultivators drives them to continue in the space. Now, with hemp offering a lifeline to many, it is unsure just how many could pivot into the sector as it heats up.

4

Manufacturing, Production, and Processing

If you are seeking a booming cannabis sector, then manufacturing, production, and processing are some of your prime options. Manufacturing, production, and processing careers offer a wide variety of options, including working with proprietary technology that is continuously furthering innovation. In turn, both medical patients and recreational users have benefitted from the ever-evolving market.

On a macro level, innovation has made medical cannabis treatments more efficient, while adult-use consumers experience more natural, flavorful highs from an assortment of oils and other consumption methods. But that would be broad generalizations of both. Extraction technology has opened up how cannabis can be extracted, isolated, injected, and consumed thanks to the specificity of numerous companies' technology.

These companies have not only excelled at research and development, but are also topping the lists of most profitable companies that major investment firms would like to have in its portfolio. Those names include Tilray, one of Canada's largest cannabis producers. In early 2019, Tilray expanded its effort to the burgeoning hemp market. It was just one of many companies that continues to do so.

In other Canadian news, Aurora and Canopy Growth, two of the largest names in the industry, are among the numerous to expand into Europe and Central America. Meanwhile, China issued licenses for growing industrial cannabis as well. In South America, most nations have passed laws, with countries like Colombia making great strides for a fraction of the production costs in North America.

With such expansion, the market can be crowded—though many note that proprietary products and patents allow for more room to breathe than what may appear. Yet, at this time, many of these products and patents are unheard of to the public. As such, these new and unique methods need to reach the public's awareness. Some companies remain limited due to regulations and budgets, often leaving marketing budgets depleted as product development remains essential. So while the tech advances, the public remains unaware.

Jill Thomassian, COO of Metagreen Ventures, a manufacturer of extraction, oil recovery and remediation machines, pointed out how important it will be to stay ahead of the competition as more massive, well-established corporations enter the CBD and THC oil production markets. Thomassian explained that "the industry is becoming more acceptable to high-value researchers that will continue to innovate novel solutions that we must stay ahead of in our own internal research and development."

When I asked Thomassian which markets in the sector would be in demand as the industry matures, she told me it's cannabis as a whole which is on the rise. "For the oil production, I believe that industrial scale, megaton factories will start to rise and dominate the recreational market." She added, "I think on the CBD side, we will start seeing FDA/GMP type factories dominate." Concerning the industry at large, she believes branded products will start to rise, "and that educated consumers will start to cause a pull market for the product mix."

Her assessment appears to be true when looking at typical job boards. ZipRecruiter.com listed almost 1,400 cannabis processing jobs as of February 2019, with positions including Lab Technicians in Adelanto, California, who can earn $14 to $16 per hour. Additional roles included extraction and distillation techs in California, who could make between $30,000 and $60,000 annually—with full benefits included. Higher up the ladder, there are Extraction Lab Manager roles which can net a person between $65,000 and $90,000.

The booming extraction sector offers opportunity and sizable incomes for those qualified, including lab director roles in areas like Washington state and Nevada, which could earn someone over $100,000, as my research in the Winter of 2019 produced.

Other jobs posted include chemist positions in North Carolina and post-processing assistants in Illinois just to name a few. Openings extended to manufacturing, where operations facilities and general managers jobs are needed for medical cannabis production in smaller towns in New York State.

Megan Archer, Director of Lab and Extraction Operations for IESO, an Illinois-based medical company, pinpointed specific careers that are in demand. "Good scientists and good researchers," she noted. "Good medicine begins with proper scientific understanding. Incorporating multiple scientific disciplines into one collaborative effort creates an environment that is wired for success."

Archer also explained that high-quality extraction is on the rise in the sector. She pointed out that effective medicine is not all that the consumer seeks—their tastes evolve with the market. "People are searching for the flavor of cannabis that makes medicating an experience. I think we are moving on from the 'shatter matters' mentality and instead focusing on terpene content and obtaining more complete plant profiles. In addition, we have also put a focus on the nuances of extraction and dialing in methods to maximize throughput while also providing quality medicine."

While manager and director roles are indeed lucrative, Archer noted another area which could provide higher career earnings. "By far, the most lucrative role would be consulting—especially if you know what you're talking about." She explained how the process of learning about the industry can be an experience in and of itself. "People are always searching for the information that will make them the best of the best. Unfortunately, with every good there is bad, and there are plenty of people out there pretending to know what they're talking about to make a quick buck."

Anthony Franciosi of Honest Marijuana Company in Colorado noted that clean consumption will only become more of a demand as the industry matures. "A solid blunt is never going to go out of style," Franciosi explained, "but it is not practical on the way to a meeting or to work for most people. Full spectrum oils and nano-tech are going to allow balanced, high-quality medicine to be delivered efficiently orally and topically with better results in the very near future."

The diverse needs of the three-pronged sector certainly drive up the demand for talent. While some training and education is ideal, a person can enter the field at any age. Many will make the jump from tangential industries, while others may find opportunity right out of college.

This is a strategy IESO is able to use thanks to its beneficial location to one of the state's top colleges, Southern Illinois University. Archer explained why the company taps into recent graduates to fill its positions. "I find that individuals fresh out of college are the best employees because they are blank slates and have unrelenting motivation." The company casts a wide net during its search, which includes looking for a variety of potentially hirable intangibles. Archer noted that IESO posts its job listings on major search websites, targeting a variety of skill sets. "Not only do we target scientists and other individuals with a large knowledge basis, but we also target hustlers like servers, baristas, and factory workers."

The rise of sourcing from college should continue in numerous parts of the country as colleges and universities open classes, minors, and majors geared toward the cannabis industry.

Whether coming from college or another walk of life, a job seeker would be wise to be well-informed of the sector's current events.

For Thomassian and MetaGreen, a hot topic has been the often murky and evolving set of regulations a company must adhere to so it remains compliant. She noted how this was the case in California. "With the passing of recreational use in California, the licensing requirements lagged the market. This resulted in quickly changing and sometimes unclear requirements at both the local and state level." This becomes even more of a concern if a company deals with THC and CBD, as MetaGreen does. "Our company is focused on both CBD and THC production, through a subsidiary, and the regulations for the two different areas conflict at times, requiring different operating procedures for the two entities."

Archer explained that a major topic of the cannabis industry—terpenes—has been all the rage in IESO's circle. "Preserving the terpene profile throughout the entire extraction and post-processing is a primary focus of our jobs." She elaborated, "Optimizing terpene profiles can be accomplished by acquiring the proper technology and technique, followed by paying extra attention to detail."

She also noted how it is a personal hot topic which could come in handy to similar job seekers with a passion for such technology. "As a classically trained analytical chemist, analytical chemistry and robust data sets have been a hot topic on my mind since first entering the cannabis space." Archer explained how this could positively serve the industry. "This realm of chemistry can benefit and provide information about each portion of the cannabis production process, from growing to product formulation."

Numerous pros and a few large and looming cons are present in today's sector, according to people interviewed for this book. Thomassian explained how the newness of the industry allows professionals to shape an emerging market through their work. In addition, both she and Archer noted the industry's ability to help people as a significant benefit to the sector that not all other markets can provide. Meanwhile, other respondents indicated the cannabis-friendly atmosphere of the space.

Overall, the most-discussed pain point of the industry had to be regulations and grey market competition. Other common drawbacks of the industry were also discussed. Those included, among other subjects, commercialization and consolidation of the market.

Archer also made a note of a critical point that some tend to overlook as the rush heats up. "While there certainly is a financial benefit to this industry, if done right, we need to stop relying on cannabis as a means to balance a budget." She expanded on her point. "Some states are using this as their approach, but we cannot rely on a medicine to be the fiscal saving grace. It is a medicine, and we need this to be our primary focus. Money will follow."

Most of the companies I spoke with touted their diverse workforce, with Honest Marijuana Company mentioning its employees range in age from twenty-two to sixty-two. Though, some have had struggles finding talent despite making conscious efforts to have an inclusive and diverse staff.

Brett Fink, SVP of the Los Angeles cannabis brand Old Pal, noted how underwhelming the results have been when using recruiting services. He explained that not many firms offered candidates of color, women, or non-binary people.

On the other hand, he noted that seniors can join the field as well. However, those making career switches could struggle with the entry-level or near-entry salary many positions offer. Those who are willing to take the chance, and can afford the likely income reduction, are likely to stand out among the rest. Fink explained how an experienced sales veteran accepted an entry-level budtender position to begin earning their reputation in the industry. "I was sold when I heard all of the sacrifices this person made to get into the industry. Automatically, I could see their tenacity and immediately wanted to learn more."

It should be noted that making such a sacrifice is not feasible for everyone. Higher costs of living ranging from higher urban rental prices to student loans to having a family can hamper taking such a risk with a lower paying career change. With many major US cannabis markets offering work, the opportunity is contrasted with the fact that many of these cities are often also the most expensive to live in.

Regardless of your situation, staying up to date on the space is essential for job seekers. Thomassian explained that "They should also know that there are some companies that are opposed to the market and may turn them down for services if they know what they do." Speaking of being turned away, Archer noted how criminal records have restricted access to many. She pointed out that "Many states have legislation against hiring people with drug-related offenses, felonies, or violent crimes on their record." This is a point that many lawmakers and politicians cite as a stipulation they want to remove to improve career and industry access moving forward.

The general consensus is that working in cannabis has been an experience that subjects love. As Archer explained, "It has of course been intriguing, fun, and rewarding; I love what I do, and I wouldn't change it for the world. Science is my passion and being able to combine that with cannabis is something I never would have dreamed I would have been able to do." That said, her path in the field may not have felt like other more established industries would have allowed for.

"I was not formally trained in cannabis prior to working with it, so I had to learn how to apply the techniques I have learned as a chemist to a completely new realm. Additionally, the current medical program in Illinois is a pilot program, so we are all learning together; this means there isn't always a mutual understanding between the different sectors of the industry as a whole. These are challenges that will hopefully be ironed out over time."

Overall, the sector is ripe for opportunity, innovation, and careers. With many positions offering livable to very comfortable salaries, this is one of cannabis's most in-demand and developing sectors. The unorthodox ways of entering the market will likely fade away as more regulation and commercialization comes into play. Despite the need for additional refining in the space, this may be one of the best opportunities for the job seekers looking to find a career in cannabis.

5

Dispensaries

When one thinks about cannabis dispensary careers, it wouldn't be a surprise if their minds go to roles like budtenders, reception, and security workers. Those roles are indeed part of the team, but are far from all that there is to offer. In many states, vertically integrated businesses are law. That means a dispensary will have cultivation, delivery, processing, and all other parts of the supply chain in its operation. As such, dispensaries have a demand for highly skilled, diverse workers.

Dispensaries offer an array of career options from customer support to medical professionals to compliance and much more. Large- and small-scale operations are going to need shop managers, as well as a full sales team. In most cases, they will have much more, including a marketing manager, customer service representatives, and extraction directors as well. Strategy and marketing also play an increased importance in cannabis brand growth as regulations limit the ways a company can advertise—making creative marketing minds a must for many companies. Integrated operations will offer up numerous roles in cultivation and development as well. Additional pressing needs come from packaging. The list goes on and on.

In short, a wealth of opportunity can be found at a dispensary.

Etain is a medical marijuana dispensary brand in New York; one of the first five companies to be licensed in the state. Its Dispensary Coordinator, Catia Lopes Nunes, explained the array of roles on the Etain team. One which Lopes Nunes singled out was technicians. These employees work under the pharmacists in similar capacities, while helping educate patients on products, expectations, and additional consumption queries.

"The technician role at our dispensaries is a critical and very popular position in applicants," Lopes Nunes said. "These personnel are often times the people who our patients see and interact with the most, so finding a good fit that is both efficient—as well as conversant with cannabis and has good customer service skills—is an important balance when considering any potential hire." Other roles work together to ensure that the company remains on the right side of the rules. "Security, additionally, is a critical function of our dispensary, along with compliance in ensuring we follow best practices along with state regulations."

The sector is such an ample space that it overlaps with other areas of the industry, including cultivation, processing, and distribution to name a few. Therefore, salary breakdowns need to be analyzed by the function within the sector. For example, data from Indeed.com listed the average compliance manager salary at over $62,000 annually. Meanwhile, a product supervisor averages just over $59,000. These averages are not cannabis-specific and should be slightly higher if they follow current industry salary trends. The same should apply for most roles in the sector.

Some dispensary careers have come under scrutiny. In these cases, specific roles are seen as positions with little to no growth. While lower-paying roles like security have been mentioned, the most common position to come up is the most well-known in the dispensary: the budtender. These professionals play a central role in the in-store customer experience. Behind the scenes, they help steer the ship and continue to do so in front of customers; even when compartmentalization is rather difficult and especially when dealing with customers and patients with varying needs.

Data from Indeed.com placed the average budtender salary at $12.75 per hour, or $26,520 if the person worked a full-time schedule all 52 weeks of the year. Budtender job listings on ZipRecruiter.com showed that salaries varied slightly depending on the market. A budtender in San Francisco could earn $16 to $18 an hour, while one in Portland listed for $13.50. In Denver, one position listed between $12 and $21 per hour.

Concerning the position, Heidi Fikstad, owner of the Eugene, Oregon–based dispensary Moss Crossing, noted a problematic balance that comes with a sometimes low-paying position. "Budtenders are not medical professionals, and there is a dance you must be able to do when trying to help a client, in which you are not giving actual medical advice, but still trying to lead them to something that may offer them relief."

With such little room for earning a comfortable living, some have wondered if the position is worth pursuing. In 2018, Mike Adams discussed the subject in his *Forbes* article, "Marijuana Employment: Is The Budtender Position A Dead End Job?" Adams addressed the budtender salary in a time of wage fights in America. "Although $16 per hour is a better wage than other, traditional dead-end jobs, like washing dishes or taking orders at McDonald's, there could come a time real soon when this is not exactly the case," Adams wrote. "Sure, the federal minimum wage is still only $7.25 per hour, but there is a push in some parts of the country to raise the minimum wage to the $15 mark. Many states and cities have already made a move."

The role being a dead end is a notion Fikstad completely disagrees with. She told me that given where the industry is, there is excellent potential in the role. She noted cannabis educator and industry consultant Emma Chasen as a perfect example. Fikstad described Chasen as someone "who had an inherent curiosity about cannabis and the science behind it. She wanted the rest of the staff she was working with to be able to speak knowledgeably about what she was learning, so she created an internal education system for her dispensary."

Chasen's career grew thanks to speaking gigs and podcast appearances. This led to creating her own dispensary teaching business. Fikstad added, "Her career path was launched from a starting position of budtender, so there ya go. Being the point person interacting with customers day in and day out gives you incredible insight into what the market is looking for, and what needs are unmet." A lasting lesson Fikstad shared could be applied to any sector: "If you can come up with a solution to meet those needs, you could be headed straight to the top."

Others may view Chasen as an outlier instead of the norm. For those, there is a legitimate concern around budtending and other careers becoming a dead end. And while it is indeed a concern, some dispensaries do strive to promote from within their ranks. Etain endeavors to do just that. Lopes Nunes explained that "Many of our management started out as customer service representatives, technicians, or receptionists." She explained why the company believes in loyalty to its team. "As the company grows, we are committed to helping our employees succeed and hope to reciprocate their commitment to us by advancing their careers when possible."

Finding work in the cannabis industry can often boil down to networking or finding a diamond-in-the-rough opportunity on job boards, though the latter is improving on select platforms. That isn't necessarily the case with dispensary careers, however. More often than not, job postings pop up on cannabis job boards like Vangst and can be found on traditional job boards with ease. Today, it is not uncommon to find dispensaries listed on LinkedIn, Indeed.com, or other popular job searching platforms.

Depending on the role, a degree or certification may be required. Cultivators, extractors, and others may need a bachelors or equivalent education. However, most positions have on-site training and are attainable for anyone with a passion for the plant. At Etain and plenty of other dispensaries, it interviews applicants of varying backgrounds. "The vast needs of each dispensary make jobs accessible for anyone interested in the cannabis industry, whether or not they have the prior education and certificates, such as a pharmacy degree," said Lopes Nunes, adding, "There are many options for employment at a dispensary."

An applicant can gain a leg up on the competition by being

informed. "Educating yourself on your state's regulations and mandated practices will be an invaluable asset when entering the industry," she noted.

Beyond traditional applications, getting involved in the community is still an effective way of getting in front of company decision makers. Lopes Nunes noted that "our dispensaries and employees are actively engaged in community outreach, education, and promotional activities." She noted that such activities also serve as another avenue for job candidates to get involved in the cannabis community and potentially connect with employers.

This approach can be beneficial to dispensaries, as well as job seekers. In markets like Hawaii, the expensive price of acquiring out-of-state talent makes recruiting extremely difficult, as Helen Cho, director of strategy at Aloha Green, told me. Cho added that the lure of leaving the island for better job prospects has created a brain drain of sorts.

Beyond the careers themselves, the dispensary sector is one buzzing with the news ranging from mergers and acquisitions to booming sales figures. Due to its overlap with so many sectors, dispensaries often have similar issues to cultivators, testing facilities, sales, and marketing (among other areas of cannabis). In addition to these topics, the dispensary space is able to continually drum up its own news.

Much of the conversation centers on the positive aspects. In both medical and recreational markets, additional dispensaries are opening. Patients and adult-use consumers now have improved access to their preferred products and medicine.

* * *

In some cases, dispensaries now represent promise for communities. This thinking typically extends from racial and socio-economic equality efforts made by activists and lawmakers. In Massachusetts, its legalized market rollout has been, in large part, considered a success. However, others insist that it has not been accessible to minority entrepreneurs and communities most impacted by the failed "War on Drugs."

In March 2019, former Boston City Councilor Tito Jackson explained to WBUR that neighborhoods in the city were perfect examples. He cited the neighborhood of Mattapan, where 90 percent of its residents are non-white, with three-quarters being black. To counter the problems, Jackson and others in similar markets are attempting to open dispensaries in these locations. Doing such a thing is easier said than done. In Boston, only two provisional licenses were given to minority-owned businesses at the time of the WBUR article.

Jackson noted the high hurdles set to qualify for a license. "The problem, really, is the barrier to entry is about a million dollars per store," he explains. "And understand, this is an industry that is un-banked. You can't go to the bank down the street and ask for a loan, because it's not federally legal." To get his capital, Jackson's company turned to a Canadian firm.

While states struggle to correct decades of past wrongdoings, its efforts to date are showing gains across the country, and the sector is buzzing over the news. States like Pennsylvania and Oklahoma show how the demand for cannabis is in no way relegated to the coasts and Colorado. Pennsylvania has fast become a darling of the industry for its enrollment of over 100,000 patients before the end of its first year. Meanwhile, Oklahoma's medical cannabis market with uncapped licenses boomed, with sales surpassing $7 million in February alone.

With gains in the industry come additional concerns. Or, as the late Notorious B.I.G. so famously said, "Mo money, mo problems." One that has continued to linger, and was discussed in further detail in the financial services chapter, is banking. At the time of this book's printing, the United States still does not allow banks to work with the cannabis industry thanks to federal tax code 280-E. This leaves dispensaries with millions in cash to pay to local and federal agencies. Dispensary owners hate it. So does the government. And with hope, this could change sooner than later. With the historic Senate hearings on cannabis banking in 2019, the US may finally be ready to tackle this long-pressing topic for dispensaries and all other touch-the-plant cannabis businesses.

The industry's growth signaled other news and happenings that got the market talking. One such case is the March 2019 dispute between two dispensaries operating under the same "Harvest" name. Both the California- and Arizona-based Harvest have claims to the trademark. The California entity has a state trademark dating back to June of 2018, while the Arizona Harvest, the one making more headlines in the industry at this time, possesses a federal trademark obtained back in 2017.

Other pressing topics that represent the industry's maturation is mergers and acquisitions. In a bid to obtain a larger market share across the country, mega players in the space purchase licenses from other entities so that it can gain a foothold in a market it otherwise couldn't due to current regulations. These entities are called multi-state operators (MSOs) and will likely become the name brands in cannabis over time. In the US, they include names like MedMen and Curaleaf.

This was a long-expected outcome that has happened for some time in the space. Now, as the revenue and investments uptick, an increased number of M&As have taken place as of late. That includes the previously mentioned Curaleaf, who acquired California's Eureka Holdings for $30.5 million as part of its aggressive country-wide expansion efforts. With numerous others doing the same across the country, there is a fear that only a few big names will remain.

* * *

Dispensary careers certainly offer a mixed bag. For Lopes Nunes, her experience in the space has been largely positive. "The pros definitely outweigh the cons for working in a dispensary." Despite its hardships, dispensaries offer ample opportunity for employment and growth in most roles. As Lopes Nunes described, "There's an abundant amount of knowledge that one will acquire—about the products, about the history of cannabis, and about the industry and the differences between each state." She went on to detail the value in customer interaction as well. "It is a rewarding and dynamic experience, and we always value the gratitude and appreciation our patients experience when using our products or visiting our dispensaries."

Lopes Nunes did note that shifting regulations keep workers on their toes. Additionally, the only clear-cut con she mentioned was the lack of transferability. "Each organization and each state implements their regulations, products, and practices differently," she explained. "Everything is so new in the cannabis industry nationwide that the skills learned at one dispensary might not apply to practices held in another state."

Depending on the role, job seekers hoping to enter the dispensary space should find a rather open market with ample opportunity. This should continue as states expand their markets, and as new states join the fold. At Etain, it hopes that New York's continued growth leads to expanded opportunities at its dispensaries and its manufacturing and cultivation facilities.

Despite the ample opportunities, job seekers should remember the potential pitfalls of the sector. Those not willing to work in the start-up space may want to skip applying. Lopes Nunes explained that the most valuable team members are those able to roll with the punches without losing their passion.

Fikstad reminded me that the industry is still quite young. Her advice to job seekers would be, "If you see this as an opportunity to build something new or find your way into an interesting new career, you will be far more likely to succeed." She added that retail experience still won't prepare a person for all the rigors of working in a dispensary. "I'd also like to again stress the importance of education and empathy. This is not your average retail job, and there is an expectation that budtenders know a lot about cannabis. That includes the science behind it, which is developing every day, and its effectiveness as a treatment for a large variety of conditions."

6

Distribution and Delivery

Distribution has long been an essential cog in the cannabis supply chain. Be it the illicit market, the mainstream, or on the delivery side, distribution has played a significant part in getting cannabis to the consumer. Now, as the market shifts, its importance has spawned off a sector of its own—and rightly so. Yet, it is a market with some struggles. Namely, the illicit market. Like cultivation, illicit market distribution has and will continue to operate alongside the legal market for the foreseeable future.

The legal side of the market began to take shape just a few years ago, as entrepreneurs saw an opportunity to thrive in the cannabis business without producing or touching any of it themselves. Detractors have called these ancillary services unnecessary middlemen. Vince Ning, co-founder of the California distributor company Nabis, pushes back on this assertion. He pointed toward the value distribution services bring to a company.

"The common misconception is that cannabis distribution does not provide value, as we are merely a middleman. However, the primary argument against that is that it is, indeed, more economical to use a third-party distributor than to self-distribute," said Ning. "Self-distribution," he elaborated, "requires an exorbitant amount of capital expenditure into fleets of trucks and warehousing just for themselves, whereas third-party distributors invest in that infrastructure for at least dozens of brands. This creates tremendous economies of scale since the volume of products lowers the average costs per delivery." Those looking for other examples of this success can look to restaurants that deliver. This extension of their service keeps many in business when they otherwise would not likely do so.

Numerous other reasons exist as well. Many opt for a distributor to cut down on time and management. In other cases, the driving (no pun intended) factor is to have such a vital component of the job in the hands of a specialist. Whatever the case may be, the need helped spawn dozens of companies in short order in markets like California.

Also in California, the illicit market continues to chug along. For decades, flower and other product has gone across the state—and more often across state lines. As the market shifted to medical and then adult use, illicit market distribution has been minimized to a degree. Though, due to regulations, costs, and other pain points in the state's adult-use infrastructure, the illicit market continues to provide a career to many. As legalization began in 2018, illegal delivery services ran amok.

Ning and Nabis operate on the legal side of the distribution market. After starting in distribution, the company expanded to cover logistics, sales, marketing, education, and other business services. Prior to entering cannabis, Ning worked as an engineer at Microsoft and later founded the company Scaphold, which was acquired by Amazon.

Ning noted that there is a strong need for distribution careers, pointing out the roughly 150,000 full-time workers employed in cannabis. On the Nabis website, it listed job positions in late winter 2019. One such role included part- and full-time drivers in Oakland and Los Angeles. The other was a full-time sales associate in the same two regions. Wages for each role change frequently and can vary by person, Ning pointed out.

Like Nabis, plenty of the major distributors now offer a range of services. In some cases, distribution is added on later as the company expands. Regardless of the process, additional positions include compliance leaders and logistics experts. Other careers in branding, warehouse management, and transportation are also possibilities.

One of the major brands to add distribution later on to its offerings is KushCo. Starting out as Kush Bottles, the company began by providing packaging to the industry in 2010. Over the years, its acquisitions and expansions have allowed it to become KushCo, branching into verticals like distribution. In 2018, the company announced the opening of a 13,000-square-foot distribution facility to serve Nevada.

In March 2019, KushCo listed 31 job openings on its website. Of them, they included roles in distribution—including warehouse manager and hazmat driver.

Numerous other high earners in cannabis are expanding through mergers and acquisitions. One such example is the Canadian company Aphria, who has partnered with Great North Distributors to be their exclusive distributor.

Canadian products are also crossing the border into the US thanks to distribution deals with certain states. With each agreement, Canadian producers are able to sell their THC and CBD products to some of the most lucrative markets in the world.

As such, the demand for distribution workers appears to be growing. Leadership positions include traditional executive roles, as well as those geared toward operations, partnerships, procurement, and other vital components of distribution. Meanwhile, sales, marketing, and account executives are all needed to maintain the relationships distributors rely on to stay in business.

While career opportunities are available on the legal side of the market, the illicit market is fading. That does not mean the black market isn't an issue for the mainstream. "The black market is looming large and is a major problem still. Estimates say that the illicit market is still three times the size of the legal market," Ning pointed out. In California, regulations appear to be the culprit once again. "It's indirectly fueled by the high tax rates imposed by local and state governments, causing the retail cost of product to the consumer to be higher than the price of product in the illicit market. In addition, the cost of compliance is lower, since there frankly isn't any in the black market."

Along with Canada's well-funded companies taking over businesses in the US, Ning sees the reduction of the illicit market as one of the most pressing topics in the space. He, like many others, believes the answer could come in lowering taxes. While California has mulled over several tax changes since beginning its adult-use market, no changes were official as of this book's publishing.

"Casey," a delivery service owner in an American illicit market, says that adult-use regulations in California are so restrictive that the illicit market seized on the opportunities; they include creating illegal marketplaces where flower and other products are sold at market rate. Outside of the state is where most of the business occurs, especially in those like California. "For the most part," Casey explained, "it's being shipped across state lines."

People often get involved in the illicit market for several reasons, including the need for fast money or to rebel against a typical lifestyle. If they find themselves caught up in the system, this short-term decision could lock them in forever. "When you're producing things in California and selling them in New York, everywhere in between is your federal crime scene," explained Casey. As such, if a person is arrested and establishes a rap sheet, then illicit market work may be their only viable option going forward. "If you get a felony for cannabis distribution, one of the only things you can continue to do is distribute cannabis," they noted. "You're not going to go out and get a job after you got a large-scale felony. It's hard."

In some instances, the legal side of the market isn't faring much better with law enforcement either. A September 2018 incident in California caught the sector's attention when two compliant distributors, working for the licensed brand Eureka, were arrested by Del Norte County California Highway Patrol. Three months later, a class-action lawsuit was filed in an attempt to block officers from seizing product and/or money from a compliant entity. The suit wasn't on behalf of the Eureka employees. Instead, it was another compliant company, Wild Rivers Transport, who had its employees stopped on their way back to its headquarters.

David Hua, founder and CEO of Meadow, a dispensary point-of-sale software which focuses on retail and delivery, discussed the perils of California's opt-out policy and police seizures. "There are many counties, over 60 percent, that do not have cannabis regulations or have banned cannabis in their jurisdiction." Like Nabis, Meadow is a member of the Cannabis Distributors Association (CDA), in addition to other industry leaders including Flow Kana, Mammoth Distribution, and Papa & Barkley.

Another matter concerning the sector has been vertical integration. Companies taking operations entirely in-house cut down on the need for distributors and full-service operations. While this alone will not end the sector, the market could see a shortage of opportunities through the constant stream of mergers and acquisitions that have continued to ramp up each year.

Hua said that while companies will condense, the industry itself will continue to generate careers. He cited a March 2019 Bureau of Labor Statistics report that the cannabis industry created 211,000 full-time jobs in the US.

Meanwhile, illegal delivery services took a significant hit in California when state-wide cannabis delivery was approved as part of the final regulations for its adult-use marketplace. The rule is widely supported by the cannabis industry. Numerous points were cited for its support, such as that, due to local regulations, some citizens are situated more than 160 miles away from the closest legal dispensary. This has been referred to as a "cannabis desert." Not everyone sees it that way. Opponents of the measure believe that the law transcends local regulations banning legal cannabis.

In making the move, some assume illegal services will see a significant hit to their market. Despite the move, don't expect to see them fold just yet. With sky-high prices, legal cannabis in California is still too expensive for many.

Overall, Hua considered the topic contentious. He explained the political uncertainty of the issue and how the illicit-market benefits. "The regulations of the Bureau of Cannabis Control allows for statewide delivery and was approved by the Office of Administrative Law. On the other hand, local municipalities believe they have control over regulating cannabis in their jurisdiction through Prop 64. While the state and local governments figure this out, illicit operators are still running." He went on to note that the only way to stop the illicit market was through competition by lowering taxes as well as producing high-quality, lab-tested products.

While the state may hope that its delivery policies end illicit market deliveries, Ning was not so sure that can happen at this time. Despite the law attempting to remedy the cannabis desert issue, Ning mentioned how it could come at too steep of a price for consumers. "I think it's still far off as no retail delivery service has state-wide scale yet and there are still gaps in the market for distant places that don't have a lot of volume of product being delivered there." He added, "This means that cost of delivery to those far-reaching regions will be very high and leaves room for a fragmented market of hyper-localized delivery services."

With such conflicts, the illicit market is likely to continue employing individuals for some time. Even when the legal market has a stranglehold on the industry, expect the illicit market to keep finding gasps of air. Due to prices and accessibility, a shortage of opportunity is likely to exist for distributors and small-time delivery-type services. In this case, Casey looks for people with an interest and a passion. From there, they aim to accommodate that person's goals within the space.

At Nabis, Ning and his team search for raw intellectual talent. While experience is a bonus, cannabis industry newcomers are welcome to apply. "They don't need to have worked in cannabis before," Ning explained. "But they need to understand our mission to be the largest distributor of cannabis products and be a part of helping us drive that goal forward."

Both sides of the market understand that cannabis is only going to become more mainstream. Companies like Nabis now position themselves to capitalize on the boom in the US and beyond. While the job opportunities do not appear to be as plentiful as other sectors of the cannabis market, distribution will play a huge factor in the growth of numerous companies. Unless they are able to make the costly decision of going in-house, companies will need to rely on third-party partners. As the market matures, so should the need for additional workers in the space.

Job seekers hoping to stay up on the sector should continue to follow developments in state regulations. Be sure to also keep tabs on how law enforcement and distribution interact. The chance of running into the police appears to be higher in this sector than some others, and could sway some job applicants. That said, those looking to learn more about the space should look into groups dedicated to the sector, like the Cannabis Distribution Association. There, people can learn about California's key issues, learn about industry leaders, and engage with the community.

7

Testing

Market research firm The Insight Partners' *Global Testing Market to 2025* report considers the US cannabis testing sector a "global benchmark." It is one of the fastest-growing and most successful markets in the cannabis industry. The report also forecasts that cannabis testing should continue to hold this position for the foreseeable future.

The report expects significant growth between now and 2025. It noted, "The global cannabis testing market is estimated to grow at a CAGR of 11.9 percent from 2018–2025." This growth is expected to stem from the general increase in legalization efforts in both the medicinal and recreational fields.

The report also noted that new laws on compulsory testing for adult-use cannabis should send the sector into another growth phase. It lists the top players in the space as:

- Agilent Technologies
- PerkinElmer, Inc.
- Shimadzu Corporation
- SCIEX
- Merck KGaA
- Restek Corporation
- Waters
- CannaSafe Analytics
- Accelerated Technology Laboratories, Inc.
- Digipath Labs

Despite a promising future, pain points do exist, with some significantly impacting certain states. They include low investments in research and development (R&D), the effects of regulations, and the high cost of cannabis testing.

As such, the sector does not generate as much of a profit as some may assume. That said, the sector is still doing well in many states. A 2017 Lab Information Management (LIMS) for cannabis quality assurance report expanded on the subject. "Cannabis testing labs don't enjoy the huge profit margins (around 40%) that growers, sellers, and extraction labs do (200%–400%), but it's still significant."

Additionally, some in the space have used methods to offer cannabis testing services. LIMS reported, "While federal schedule-1 classification remains in place, those high-profit industry players have to do business in cash, for the most part, unable to utilize FDIC-insured banks, while independent labs can add cannabis testing to their services with no such restrictions."

Regardless of the lab, cannabis is tested for a series of information and data. Patrick Bennett wrote an incredible deep dive on the subject for Leafly in late 2018. In his article, he detailed a key area of the sector.

"The cannabis lab testing industry is mainly concerned with compliance data—these are all of the testing protocols mandated by a state's regulatory body that must be performed on a cannabis product in order for it to be approved for distribution and sale. When a cannabis product 'meets compliance' that means it meets the state's standards pertaining to pesticides, contaminants, mold, and mildew," Bennett wrote.

He explains that accredited labs use proper analytical methods to produce their data. However, there is no universal standard. Due to the scheduling of cannabis on the federal level, each state has its own protocols.

When testing cannabis, analyses tend to scrutinize:

- Potency
- Contamination
- Microbial contaminants
- Physical contaminants
- Cannabinoid profile
- Terpene profile

Job seekers can enter three general labs in the cannabis space. These labs focus on extraction, analytics, or research. However, there is no clear divider among the three, as LIMS reported:

"There is of course overlap, in that many analytical labs do their own extraction, and research labs may indeed involve the same analytical methods as an analytical lab as part of their work, and may procure testing materials and/or standards from extraction labs, etc."

LIMS went on to delve into the benefits of lab work and its growth potential. "...While extraction labs may enjoy considerable profit margins (as do growers and dispensaries/retailers) and analytical labs somewhat less so, it is still the biggest growing (no pun intended) industry in the US today, and provides ample opportunity so that many labs are adding cannabis testing to their existing services and cannabis startups are emerging at a notable rate."

Careers listed on Indeed.com and Glassdoor.com during the winter of 2019 found an array of positions available. For example, a lab director in San Diego could earn $90,000 to $110,000. Meanwhile, a Chemistry Analyst in Boulder, Colorado, could make between $18 and $22 an hour. Other roles, like a lab manager, could earn a person up to $140,000 annually while a lab tech in San Francisco can make $17 to $21 per hour.

Eleanor Kuntz, PhD, is the CEO of LeafWorks, an herbal genetics company that creates verification tools for cultivators. She sees the need for testing professionals growing as the industry moves further toward compliance. She pointed out a growing demand for chemists and geneticists, as well as individuals with both cannabis and business experience. "There is still a lack of organizations in place to service the growing testing needs of the community and marketplace," Dr. Kuntz explained.

Shanel Lindsay, the founder and president of the Massachusetts-based cannabis decarboxylation company Ardent Cannabis, also sees the demand rising as the market grows in each state. "The testing laboratories aren't testing anything out of state. They're just testing within the state," she pointed out. In her home state, its market is growing and thriving. As such, its testing sector grows along with it. "Just look at the cultivation and processing, and you'll see how many testing labs you need."

With demand fluctuating by state, Lindsay is hesitant to call the sector booming. However, she did say, "I think it's an incredibly important and stable part of the industry." One area that could be expanding within testing is going beyond traditional labs. This is an area especially of interest to Ardent's founder. With at-home analysis, the cannabis community's access to accurate testing expands beyond the lab and for businesses that can afford it.

She considers at-home testing the next frontier. With the increasing rise of personal growers, the need for an affordable in-home solution is imperative. "There's a huge desire for people to be able to quantify and know what is in whatever that they're growing, that they encounter," she explained, adding, "that just does not exist right now."

Lindsay also noted a series of additional needs in the industry. They included optimizing the grow process, as well as DNA testing and its biological profiles.

Brad Bogus, VP of Growth & Marketing at Confident Cannabis, an information and management system used by 40 percent of labs nationwide, is another person who sees room for growth in the sector. "Almost every state requires testing for their market to operate; that's definitely not going to go away on the federal level. Testing is only going to increase from here."

Bogus also noted that shifting regulations have hampered growth, especially in some adult-use states. For example, he cited California's shifting regulations that cost companies large sums to remain compliant and operational. "You have a lot of licensees who are struggling or going out of business, therefore not testing their product. So the labs will suffer down the chain as a result of that. So, in a lot of these states, there's a squeeze. Labs feel it when there's a squeeze, and that might temporarily suspend the growth of that sector of the market for a little bit."

This is the current situation in Oregon, he pointed out, where oversupply is the culprit and a backlog of tested flower goes unsold. However, he did point toward positive efforts in Massachusetts, as well as Michigan. "I think the labs are doing really well there. They're experiencing that first stage boom and have been able to learn a lot from the Oregons of the world."

Needless to say, the sector is brimming with pressing topics to discuss. From innovations to regulations, the market is filled with current events which could impact the short- and long-term outlook of the space. The Insight Partners report noted vital market dynamics, such as the legalization of medical cannabis across the world.

It stated, "This has become the driving force for the growth of cannabis testing marked in the entire North America region. Currently, [there are] more than 8,000 active licenses for cannabis businesses in the USA. It is the only country with such a number of market players. Europe is another region which has shown a decent growth rate for cannabis testing market. There has been an increase in the process of legalization of cannabis in European countries. In November 2018, the government of the UK announced that medicinal cannabis is legal. The main force for growth in demand of cannabis is because of the use of cannabis in pesticides in Europe. The growing number of cannabis testing laboratories have fueled the demand for cannabis in the European region."

The Asia Pacific region also stands to be a growing influence, with Thailand being the first country in Asia to legalize medical use in 2018. While only a blip of the region's radar, the news could spark other countries in the surrounding area to follow suit if the results and the revenue prove worthy.

Other talking points involve the opportunities that arise thanks to the signing of the US Farm Bill. That includes Canadian companies like FluroTech, which recently aimed to expand into the US. In a March press release, the company stated that "With the U.S. Federal legalization of hemp, FluroTech is able to expand its addressable market in North America to the U.S. and progress its goal to be the preferred in-house precision testing device for hemp and cannabis growers globally," commented FluroTech CEO Danny Dalla-Longa.

Groundbreaking technology could emerge in the form of THC breathalyzers. Hound Labs, a breath diagnostics company, had its second positive clinical trial back in February 2019. As *Mashable*'s Chris Taylor explained, this technology may advance testing but could pose ethics questions between law enforcement and the public. "Even if Hound Labs' tech is for real, even if it can show exactly how much THC entered your system in the last couple of hours, it's easy to see scenarios where cops might abuse it for an easy arrest of a non-impaired driver, or employers might use it to safely get rid of the long-haired guy they just don't like."

All things considered, the need for cannabis testing professionals is growing. Those with lab experience can likely make the transition into the field. Keep in mind that certain education and career backgrounds are likely to be required for most roles.

As the Insight Partners report notes, conferences are on the rise as well. This highlights the burgeoning demand for cannabis and the growth of specific sectors. Many conferences are beginning to be tailored to niche areas of the market. Those hoping to network with the testing community may want to consider an event like the Analytical Cannabis Expo in San Francisco. At the three-day event, extraction, science, and testing all take center stage.

The event focuses on scientific research, testing, regulations, and encouraging collaboration and innovation in the space. Additionally, networking is a prime focus of the three-day affair.

As its website explains, "With assistance from our expert advisory board, we have put together an agenda that will ensure you hear from the leaders that are dedicated to driving the cannabis industry forward. For anyone interested in cannabis testing, extraction, regulation, and consumer safety this is a must-attend event."

A number of personalities and skill levels can enter the sector, though some traits are ideal to go along with a person's work experience. Many noted the need for enthusiasm in the industry, a uniform ideal heard across cannabis. Additionally, a willingness to look at complex problems with fresh vision is a highly sought-after trait.

In our chapter on tech, Ardent's Lindsay dove into a particular set of skills needed in cannabis. She mentioned that, as the industry is largely a startup space, flexibility is crucial. The ability to think more like a partner rather than an employee helps show leadership that you are the type of person to solve problems in a sector that often doesn't have time to get involved with anyone else's workload.

Those hoping to enter into the testing field should find ample opportunities to find a career. The outlook of each state impacts its need for testing facilities and careers. As a whole, the demand for more labs and professionals is growing, even in struggling markets.

"The testing sector is just opening up. There is a lack of data and resources to do good science," explained Dr. Kuntz. "As cannabis becomes more normalized, and formal research programs at universities and in the private sector become more established, there will inevitably be a large amount of novel discovery and data generated. The lack of agricultural and medical research is a direct result of prohibition and lack of access to the plant and persons using the medicine."

8

Financial Services and Insurance

Financial services are booming in cannabis. From full-service firms to boutique businesses, numerous companies provide ventures with the finance and guidance needed to steer a path to success in the burgeoning market.

A service starting to grow is the complex insurance space. Everyone needs to protect their business but that protection is far from one-size-fits-all. With the current regulations in the United States, insurance providers may be the only safety net some ventures have at their disposal. However, federal regulations usually limit the amount of providers offering coverage to cannabis busi-nesses. Often, options are limited to wholesalers and not major insurance companies. This could change if the recent federal hearings prompt any legislative changes.

This sector offers a wide variety of career opportunities, most of which can be rather lucrative—even at entry-level salaries.

The first role that may come to mind is a stockbroker, which would be a fair starting point for this area of the industry. As more companies are publicly traded in the American and foreign markets, the need for trusted cannabis investment professionals grows exponentially. Traditional brokerages like Charles Schwab Fidelity track the activity of marijuana ETFs and major pub-licly traded players like Aurora, Tilray, MedMen, and other top names in the space.

Meanwhile, the rise of app-based investment tools like Robinhood have opened up a new avenue where the broker isn't needed, but a tech team is necessary to support the app. As such, opportunities could be on the rise at the intersection of tech and finance.

Those with a knack for the market could find work as an ana-lyst or research associate. These roles require a thorough analy-sis of the industry's daily workings. The need for this sort of employment can be found within high-earning cannabis compa-nies, as well as research groups and financial services firms.

A number of financial companies in the cannabis sector also include "brokerage" in its list of services. Other services tend to include advising, asset management, 401k and profit-share plan-ning. Instead of focusing on a single aspect of financial services, larger-scale organizations offer a plethora of assistance in an array of financial fields. Some specialists include experts of cannabis tax codes, namely section 280E.

Jill Thomassian, COO of Metagreen Ventures, mentioned how difficult it has been to find accounting professionals—especially in regard to the federal tax code. "With the 280E tax, it is important to understand cost accounting concepts to properly load COGs. In general, it has been very difficult to attract accounting professionals to the industry."

Banking and legal experts are also in demand, as are advisors in mergers and acquisitions, a trend that is rapidly gaining in the industry. Other high-interest job experience may include consulting, real estate, and payroll management.

Other companies focus on a particular aspect of the space. This can include debt collection and accounts receivable, like the work done by CannaBIZ Collects. Managing partner Brett Gelfand noticed the need for sales and finance professionals across the board. "Since cannabis is still young and heavily relationship-based, it is key to find salespeople that not only understand the industry but may also have existing contacts and networks that can benefit your top line." The twenty-four-year-old CEO added, "We also are seeing a rise in demand for experienced, financial professionals that can better manage and oversee canna-companies' cash flow and financial trajectory."

Some financial firms also offer insurance as part of their package of services. In other cases, cannabis insurance providers work as a standalone service. Looking at the insurance market, it becomes clear why standalone services are viable.

Each cannabis sector has its own needs and concerns when seeking insurance coverage. The same can be said of lawyers, retailers, and the entire hemp industry as well. To cover the needs of each, insurance companies tend to offer a variety of products that include everything from liability to crops to data breaches. As such, the staff of a cannabis insurance firm can require an array of specialists in a number of product specialties to meet consumer demands. The market can also open the need for leadership, like a director of underwriting.

With the federal tax code restricting traditional banking services, the industry has created its own sector to combat one of its largest pain points. There are a number of platforms and methods employed; some automate cash handling for businesses while others protect investments with turnkey systems. In all, these services aim to bring some semblance of regular banking to the industry. In doing so, the hope is that the market will become safer as a whole. That includes lowering the risk of a business being robbed, as well as curbing acts like money laundering.

It would be remiss to overlook financial executives and decision makers as well. Bryan Passman, founder of cannabis industry search firms The GIGG (for staffing) and Hunter + Esquire, noted a high demand for such leaders. "As cannabis companies grow to a certain level where it no longer makes sense to outsource financial functions, they begin to create in-house roles such as CFO, controller, treasurer, etc.," explained Passman. When it comes to adding other staff, it can depend on a company's earnings.

"Many cannabis companies can do their own basic bookkeeping up until the $100k–$250k range, then things can get more technical for our industry and professional expertise is required." Prior to reaching this threshold, the need for outsourced financial services presents an opportunity that many companies are competing for.

Those looking to enter the space can do so by climbing up the ranks, or by making a lateral move. In either case, a series of soft skills, tech know-how, and certifications can help a person land a job in cannabis. Robert Half's 2019 accounting and finance salary guide may help job seekers, though the information is not geared to marijuana specifically. According to the report, hot positions in the space include:

- Accounting manager
- Controller
- Financial analyst
- Internal auditor
- Payroll manager
- Senior accountant
- Staff accountant

Some of the most sought-after tech skills include:

- Artificial intelligence
- Cloud-based systems (NetSuite, Workday)
- Construction project management software
- Data analytics and database management software (SQL, VBA)
- Enterprise resource planning systems (Microsoft Dynamics GP, Oracle, SAP)
- Excel
- QuickBooks (for small and midsize businesses)
- Real estate software (MRI, Yardi)
- Robotic process automation

Meanwhile, some of the most desired certifications and degrees are:

- CPA (certified public accountant)
- CFA (chartered financial analyst)

- CFP (certified financial planner)
- CGMA (chartered global management accountant)
- CIA (certified internal auditor)
- CISA (certified information systems auditor)
- CMA (certified management accountant)
- CPP (certified payroll professional)
- Bachelor's degree in accounting or finance
- MBA (Master of Business Administration)

Activity ranging from new ventures to mergers and acquisitions to regulatory news results in a sector often flooded with news. As such, the need for financial reporting has grown with the sector.

In just a few short years, the sector has changed its hiring approaches. Robert Half's report found that companies are finding success by tapping into the contingent workforce while also relaxing the rigorous demands of the hiring process. This change in approach is needed as new standards increased the need for additional talent. As the Robert Half report notes, "As firms update technology and accounting procedures to align with these guidelines, they need employees with experience in revenue accounting, revenue reporting, and U.S. Securities and Exchange Commission [SEC] reporting."

Federal Tax Code 280E will continue to be a prime concern in the sector. Change could come on that front soon enough. Historic progress came in February 2019, when Congress asked Federal Reserve Chairman Jerome Powell about banking for the industry. Powell got the industry buzzing when he voiced his support for change. "I think it would be great to have clarity," Powell said from Capitol Hill. "It puts financial institutions in a very difficult place and puts the supervisors in a difficult place, too. It would be nice to have clarity on that supervisory relationship."

Looking at the stock markets and the need for cannabis banking only becomes more evident. This past winter saw the cannabis industry reach another milestone when the ETFMG Alternative Harvest ETF, which is headlined by significant players like Cronos, Canopy, Aurora, and Tilray, topped $1 billion in assets under management. In just two years since becoming a marijuana ETF, the only pure-play cannabis ETF trading on the market gained 50 percent, or double what the S&P returned during that window.

The needs of the industry seem to be forcing the government's hand. Policy experts seem to believe that something will happen sooner than later. Some see the odds reaching as high as 75 percent. Others place the number slightly lower, yet still remain optimistic. In February, Ryan Donovan, chief advocacy officer for the Credit Union National Association, told MarketWatch he agreed with the optimism. "Seventy-five percent may be a little high, but [the odds] are better than they were in the last Congress."

Regardless of the banking outcome, the sector is full of optimism. While significant pain points linger, the ability to grow and shape an industry outweigh the concerns for those in the space. Like numerous other cannabis sectors, there is ample room to make an impact in a shorter time than any other industry would allow. This is, in part, due to regulations holding back major players. "Since most major institutions and Fortune 500s are up against the glass watching private business and investors take advantage of the space, this allows for major upside for start-up cannabis businesses," explains Gelfand.

He also noted the drawbacks that regulations bring, which include "banking limitations, digital marketing limitations, and the quickly changing regulations cannabis companies need to stay up-to-date with." With the market moving so rapidly, he also notices many making costly errors. "As companies race to be a part of this 'green rush,' competition continues to increase, and proper business planning may be neglected which leads to default, lawsuits and high turnover."

Drawbacks exist in insurance as well. The maturing cannabis industry allows for some questionable characters to enter the space. While this is on the decline, certain services still need to be on the lookout. This is especially true for sectors where their website is often a lead generator, like insurance. Those in the space have to understand that not all queries are from viable business partners.

With the sector expanding, many see ample opportunities for growth and success. However, Gelfand made a claim for staying in your lane—at least to a degree. "Since cannabis legalization, the industry continues to become more and more competitive. It is extremely difficult to be the best in multiple sectors in this industry. By discovering a need and developing a specific solution, cannabis entrepreneurs have a high chance of success."

That said, job seekers have quite a bit to consider if they want to enter this sector of cannabis. The market is fast and high earning. Major moves happen on a frequent basis and should only ramp up as the sector evolves. While the sector is wide-reaching, it remains a small community. "Although the cannabis industry is growing, it is still a tight community to land a job at a cannabis company, you will most likely need to know a direct or indirect source that is in the industry," described Gelfand.

The need for additional professionals in the financial services and insurance community is already warming up, and should continue to grow as revenue flows into the industry and especially if federal policy changes. This can already be witnessed in the uptick in mergers and acquisitions and gains on the stock market.

To seem the most appealing to companies, job seekers should understand the growing demands of the sector and the industry at large. That includes understanding the broad strokes as well as the minute details that make up each aspect of the industry. Passman explained that "Financial services professionals should educate themselves on the cannabis industry and its challenges in general, and specifically digging into the cannabis industry's very unique financial challenges. For example, banking, or the lack thereof, and tax code difficulties."

9

Board Leaders and Executives

"A cannabis company must be agile and have a solid handle on navigating through regulations, running a business with unique challenges, staying informed at the state and local level, and creating a healthy employee work environment," explains Autumn Shelton, owner and CFO of Autumn Brands. What is true of the cannabis company begins with the people leading the organization. Today, the need for experts in company leadership and other vital decision-making positions is apparent. Without a capable and compliant leader (or leaders) at the top, a company is sure to falter.

Harborside dispensary co-founder and activist Steve DeAngelo knows this all too well. He saw how the legacy individuals—those that helped build the industry while it was an entirely or mostly illicit market—in the business often did not have the mainstream business know-how to thrive in the modern market as it came to be. "We didn't have the opportunity to develop a lot of these skill sets that are needed to be successful in today's cannabis market," the industry veteran pointed out. "If we marketed or packaged or labeled our products, law enforcement would follow those products back to us." Legacy cannabis individuals were more likely to know how to run an illegal operation, but the new reality for cannabis was quite a foreign concept.

When legalization reached California, many legacy individuals were unaware of how to seek out investors, engage with banks, or just set up a legal business structure. DeAngelo explains, "We did the best we could with the guidance that we held from the gray market, but there wasn't much of it." A need for experienced business leaders was required, and continues to grow in demand today as a growing number of cannabis companies become mega players.

It is vital to remember that cannabis replicates the rest of the market. Because of this, company leaders from virtually any walk of life can become an executive or high-level manager. In California, where the rules are often evolving, Autumn Shelton understands the importance of quality decision makers. "Regulations in California and how you interpret them have changed daily over the last year and a half. It's important to have executive leadership in every sector of the cannabis market."

Nick Kovacevich is CEO of KushCo Holdings Inc., one of

the top performing companies in cannabis today. Kovacevich echoes Shelton's sentiment that, as these young companies scale their business model and even go public, the need for top-quality executive leadership grows. He explained where his company and others seek out executives from other sectors. "You're already seeing it," he notes, adding, "GTI, KushCo, MedMen are all bringing in high-power executives from CPG, tech, and more."

Shelton and Kovacevich represent two of the varying ways a person can become a business leader in the sector. Kovacevich got into cannabis right after college, where he majored in sports management. In 2010, he co-founded what was then Kush Bottles. Since then, his company has grown into a cannabis behemoth. The company re-branded into KushCo Holdings in 2018, and then re-branded the primary business unit from Kush Bottles to Kush Supply Co.

Unlike Kovacevich, Shelton's career began in other sectors, like many in the space. After college, she earned her broker's license and worked in various real estate sectors for over a decade. In these roles, her focus was mainly on cost analysis and the returns on commercial and residential property. She explained how she translated her expertise to her partner's cut flower business and now Autumn Brands, a non-GMO, organic cannabis cultivation brand.

Numerous other entry points exist, including internal promotions. Some leaders have noted that this is an upward trend as companies develop and promote from within. This path becomes more likely as companies mature and teams solidify over the years. Another avenue is through mergers and acquisitions, a growing trend as previously mentioned. In these cases, decision makers from the acquiring company may join the board or leadership of the purchased company.

With such opportunity and fair market pay for most, Shelton sees how being an executive can create a lengthy career in the space for someone. This is especially true, as Shelton says, for "those that are involved right now and can get through all the challenges we face [as we] are paving the road for the future." That said, she did offer up a bit of caution. "No other industry has to jump through the hoops that we have to at this point in time. Not only because of the changing regulations, or that it is new, but mostly because it's still federally illegal and commerce is limited to dispensaries within their own state."

Shelton believes that those involved in the space will gain lessons and knowledge to set them apart from other executives. She does warn that the position is not for everyone. "This is not for the light of heart. There are so many hurdles to go through, that it takes real tenacity, the ability to know when to spend money and when not to."

Kovacevich discussed similar issues. He pointed out that, like any firm in a growth stage, the education, experience, and professionalism of the industry is where it needs to be. At KushCo, the company runs a booming brand, not a rag tag wannabe-cool brand you may find on sizzle reels. Some startups in and out of cannabis don't follow this path. They often find themselves in trouble with investigators and potentially even regulators thanks to a lack of oversight for a number of concerns. To avoid such an outcome, KushCo adheres to common workplace rules, including a ban on consumption of any kind in the workplace.

By having such a professional work environment, KushCo is ready to receive guests at its space; be they investors or anyone uncertain about cannabis. Being able to dispel a long-held cannabis misconception brings him and the company joy. "One of the most rewarding parts of showing people our space and having visitors interact with our employees is to push aside the notion that because we work in the cannabis space that people would be 'high' or smoking or having flower laid out everywhere. It's a business and office like any other one you would walk into."

That is the fact that not everyone outside of cannabis has picked up on just yet: Cannabis jobs are often just like regular office careers. Sure, the product may be more alluring, but cannabis is just another commodity at its core. It's a job creator and significant money maker. To keep both of those features true, it takes a dynamic team of workers to grow brands and remain compliant. While an office can be fun, it will be much like a beer or cigarette producer—people will not be consuming the "products" on company time or on-site.

Departments within cannabis mirror other major industries. Kovacevich laid out his company organization, one he said mirrors other distribution or logistics B2B businesses. He said that at KushCo, the company has a technology development team, marketing, sales, operations, warehouse, supply chain, legal, corporate development, and HR departments.

For Autumn Brands, its founder noticed the change a few years back at a major conference. "It was very clear how the cannabis market had shifted at the MJ Biz Conference 2016 in Las Vegas, where almost everyone was dressed in business attire, rather than the once perceived hippie style. Experienced business leaders understand the growth and endless opportunities of this industry." Today, her direct team is comprised of a bookkeeper, HR/compliance director, and software admin.

Ardent Cannabis CEO Lindsay, too, noticed this change. She remarked how regulations and compliance emphasize the need for every T to be crossed and every i to be dotted. Yet, that focused, type-A structure still allows for the brand to come through so that all the traditional business trappings are on display while high-quality cannabis products get produced.

While navigating the choppy waters of the industry, companies and teams continue to grow—some even more than what is mentioned above. In addition to direct team support, growing cannabis brands have everything from marketing, sales and business development roles to support like assistants, office managers, and custodial crew. As the industry grows, the replication of the traditional office space should only continue to develop further. That also includes working with contingent labor, be it freelance, contract, or seasonal talent.

While opportunity abounds, there is debate around representation at the top of the sector. Those interviewed for this book reported that they felt that adequate diversity and inclusion opportunities are happening at their companies. Some feel that this applies to the industry at large. This sentiment extends to leadership, as well as management and other office roles. Those that feel this way believe that there is equal opportunity to make an impact in the industry.

Kovacevich explained how KushCo has made efforts to include diverse backgrounds and women in leadership roles. He touted board member Barbara Goodstein, whom he described as "a highly coveted person" thanks to her senior leadership experience in operations, business, and marketing development at firms including Bankers Trust, Instinet, Vonage, and American Express.

While the rest of the KushCo board is male, the brand strives to continue its evolution. To achieve such goals, the company endeavors to empower and mentor future leaders. Kovacevich explained, "We have about 35 percent of our employee population as women and we just completed our first annual women's summit, where all women in the company are brought to HQ for a day around mentorship, panel discussion, growth, and support."

Cassandra Farrington, co-founder and CEO of *Marijuana Business Daily*, one of the premier news outlets for cannabis business, sees her sector as an example for other industries. "As any industry matures, it is going to attract more and more traditional business people. As a result, the percentage of males leading companies in the industry has indeed risen. In addition, several early-mover females have successfully exited their companies. It's no surprise that the capital available to find those exits comes from male-dominated enterprises. These enterprising and risk-taking women played a pivotal role in the development of the cannabis industry and paved the way for the industry to continue to be more inclusive and open to diversity than is traditionally seen across businesses."

Data from *Marijuana Business Daily* that the average number of female executives in cannabis has declined from 36 percent in 2015 to 26.9 percent in 2017. It should be noted that cannabis was still ahead of the 2016 national average, 23 percent, for female executives in 2016.

Additional data from Marijuana Business Daily in August 2019 saw a significant shift, with women leadership jumping 10 percent. As of the summer 2019, women hold 37 percent of executive positions in the cannabis industry. This may help ease some of the sentiments shared in recent years, while also highlighting how fast the cannabis industry can pivot on just about any subject.

Last year, I attended an a cannabis and networking series,

REVEL, in New York City where I was able to interview speakers such as former NFL running back turned investor Tiki Barber and Tahira Rehmatullah, the CFO for MTech Acquisition Corp, who is considered one of the most influential voices in cannabis today.

At the event, Rehmatullah explained to me how the industry was once more inclusive and diverse, but has now regressed as the boom meets mergers and acquisitions. Rehmatullah added how the industry was beginning to resemble others, and not in a good way. "You don't see women on boards. You don't see people of color. I think the industry has taken a couple of steps back," she told me in November 2018.

During the presentation portion of the event, Barber found himself in a not-so-ideal scenario. While showcasing his cannabis venture, Grove Group Management, on stage, Barber went to a slide of the company's management team. While a diverse group of races and backgrounds, the board was all male. The crowd pushed back rather hard for a business networking showcase. To Barber's credit, he and one detractor were able to engage on stage and discuss the matter. While nothing had changed, a civil and open discussion did occur that evening . Unfortunately, that conversation doesn't get to happen on most occasions.

Lindsay shared similar sentiments as Rehmatullah. She noted that cannabis's history with race and the failed War on Drugs impacting expectations on the nascent industry. "Our demands for inclusion and diversity within this industry go much loftier and higher than for other industries." In terms of ideals for the industry's leadership, Lindsay said, "you're looking for participation at least as equal to what the population looks like."

Varying sectors of the industry have proven to be better examples than others when it comes to diverse leadership.

Lindsay added that while some have advocated for an organic

approach to providing equal, diverse, and inclusive efforts, that is not a feasible reality. "If that's not done in an intentional way, recruiting a diverse workforce, it's not going to happen. Let's be clear, it does not happen organically. That's why you're having these conversations."

The Ardent founder noted workforce struggles in Ardent's home state, Massachusetts. "Seventy percent of the Massachusetts cannabis workforce here is a white man—probably more than that because there were 10% who refuse to answer the question [on the survey]."

While the debate rages on, Kovacevich sees the future of leadership to be diverse and woman centric. He signaled toward the generally young and open-minded business leaders situated on the more liberal coasts of the country. "Those factors all lend leadership to put more emphasis and resources to ensure the workforce at a company mirrors their own core passions and beliefs. The future involves people from the existing cannabis industry and other visionary leaders who have pioneered other industries like tech, CPG, and more and their entrance into cannabis will elevate the overall interest and execution of the work the companies in the industry are doing."

Harborside's DeAngelo thinks that cannabis "has a long way to go" on correcting its past. "The cannabis industry was created out of a society that still has roundly marginalized people of color and women. We have great opportunity in the cannabis industry to do a reset in that regard."

He explained how cannabis has to get it right now before the industry matures and solidifies. "The unique thing about this industry is it starts all at once. A law changes and everybody lines up on the start line and the whistle blows and we're off to the races. But before that, it's a blank slate. So, we get to set the norms and the standards for this industry and shame on us if all we do is build another industry that looks like every global industry that's out there today. We have an opportunity to do something differently."

To make a difference, DeAngelo says cannabis must do more than just grow as an industry. "We need to grow a new claim to the industry. The best way to make sure that we grow a new kind of industry is to make sure that a whole lot of different kinds of people are involved."

For Shelton, ideal leaders combine business acumen and cannabis appreciation. "An ideal leader in the cannabis industry is someone that has a natural sense of business and a respect for understanding every aspect of the cannabis plant." By taking on the role herself, she has learned quite a deal. "I have learned how to be 100 percent compliant in a California regulated cannabis market, yet function in a federally illegal market."

Kovacevich echoes the need for someone with business sense; namely, an entrepreneurial spirit. Additionally, an ability to go with the flow is needed in a space consumed by regulation changes. From there, an ideal leader is able to re-prioritize in real time. "There are so many variables that affect the business day-to-day that you can't control and it takes a leader who can understand that and embrace that."

A positive disposition is also needed, according to Kovacevich. "There are too many things that happen every day that can lend someone to exude negativity and that infiltrates the employee population. Leaders need to be seen under control, solutions-oriented, and that is critical to developing a culture of innovation and success."

With that in mind, he shared what he has learned to date while in the industry. Much like an ideal leader, everyone must be dynamic and capable of absorbing change. He explained:

"The creation of an industry from the ground up is unprecedented in our modern time, and I've learned it's equally important to focus on the day, executing the things you need to on a minute by minute basis to move your business forward. But you also need to spend time each day to look around the bend. This industry changes so quickly that if you don't anticipate and proactively make leaps and changes to account for what you think will happen, you will be left wondering how this opportunity passed by."

For Shelton, she learns something new each day about the benefits of cannabis. In addition to appreciating the plant more each day, she also appreciates her team. "I have learned how important an incredible team of owners, managers, and employees is to running a successful and happy business. The future leadership of cannabis is someone with successful business experience or an intrinsic quality for business and compliance."

10

Government, Law, Compliance, and Policy

Cannabis compliance is one of, if not the most, pressing issues in the industry today. For one, regulations in many parts of the country remain anything but solidified. Even in markets where cannabis is legal, its rules are known to shift. In this sector of the field, a person can help shape those laws or help companies ensure that they follow them.

In some cases on the state level, rules have been known to shift at any time. One of the most telling examples is in California. While well-intentioned and hoping to keep citizens safe from contaminants, the state is often cited for its over-regulation that stifles companies and markets. In terms of cannabis, it has been credited as the downfall for many businesses in the state. The same has happened with prices of products. In doing so, plenty of customers in California have turned back to the illicit market while businesses suffer and shut their doors under the current laws and regulations. Similar instances have led buyers in other states back to the illicit market as well.

"Right now, California's cannabis laws require a more rigorous set of compliance steps than any other products in the state," explained Harborside's DeAngelo. "We need experts who have a depth of expertise in compliance."

That compliance expertise can come from numerous career backgrounds and educations. Career opportunities exist in all sorts of roles. They can include a company compliance manager, as well as lawyers, lawmakers, regulatory specialists, and other applicable roles.

To get a look at the rising importance of cannabis policy, look no further than lobbyists on Capitol Hill. After years of cannabis being shunned by lawmakers, now it is one of the hottest topics on the Hill. While it continues to have lobbies pushing against its progress, the industry now has the revenue and power to push back. Data found on OpenSecrets.org stated that $35,000 was spent on lobbying in support of marijuana in 2011. By 2016, that number had jumped to $430,000. One year later, the sum crossed one million, totaling $1.62 million. In 2018, that number leaped to $2.5 million.

In 2018, ten reported clients lobbied for cannabis. The organizations and their totals spent were:

1. National Cannabis Industry Association: $495,000
2. New Federalism Fund: $426,316
3. Canndescent: $360,000
4. Surterra Holdings: $270,000
5. WeedMaps: $260,000
6. PalliaTech Inc: $240,000
7. Trulieve: $160,000
8. Curaleaf Inc.: $160,000
9. Cannabis Trade Federation: $140,000
10. Oregon Cannabis Association: $10,000

In total, fifty individual lobbyists worked on behalf of cannabis in 2018.

Cannabis lobbying received a significant bump in news coverage in 2019. Former Speaker of the House and anti-pot lawmaker turned Acreage Holdings board member John Boehner got involved in cannabis lawmaking. Now, instead of voting on laws, he'd be supporting the newly found lobbying group, the National Cannabis Roundtable. The news represented a further step in Boehner's about-face on the topic, as well as boost to the industry's efforts on Capitol Hill. While some may feel that Boehner's presence in cannabis is not appreciated, his expertise in lawmaking is immensely valuable to a nascent, somewhat illegal industry.

With laws being made and influenced on the national level, state and local laws are going through a similar influence. Which brings us back to the need for policy, law, and compliance experts in all sectors of the industry.

Brian Barkovitz, PE is the Principal and Director of Plumbing and Fire Protection at ABS Engineering. In addition to cannabis, ABS's work includes Shake Shack (location in Harlem, New York), Blu Dot (their Seattle flagship location) and the Lower East Side Gallery (located in Manhattan, New York), to name a few. In operation since 1983, the company recently entered into cannabis compliance by helping companies design and build facilities up to code. So far, he describes the field as "pretty competitive." Though, he noted that competition has not left the market short on businesses and jobs. "Most firms have a pretty solid niche for the type of work they do and are able to get a lot of repeat work from the same clients."

Andrew Livingston, Director of Economic and Research at the cannabis law firm Vicente Sederberg LLC, expanded on the need for compliant businesses across the burgeoning industry. "There's a lot of compliance requirements throughout and they're different." Livingston highlighted several areas of need. They include conformity around areas such as adequately tracking items, weighing product accurately, and security. He also mentioned a variety of other areas as well, including security specialists who have to structure equipment to ensure that no lines of sight are obfuscated. Indoor grow facilities can face a litany of regulation in certain jurisdictions, including fetal cell tracking, chemical and pesticide use allowed under state law, and pesticide applicator permits.

In manufacturing and extraction, Livingston noted that fire safety is a significant concern. Solvents are able to cause immense damage, including deadly home accidents by amateur growers. They can also occur in lab spaces. As such, regulations are rather high in the space. Extractors and producers have to contend with state and local fire code requirements, including blast proof doors. With such a volatile process, scores of regulation is warranted.

The retail experience has rules that most liquor store employees and consumers are accustomed to. The industry has numerous other regulations on the state and local level. Livingston pointed out common compliance parameters including sale tracking, inventory management, security, and restricting sales to only people aged twenty-one and over. Each are essential to retail ventures remaining compliant and growing their brands. In the early days of the market, the last thing a thriving dispensary—or the industry—needs is cannabis being sold to minors or unregulated items being consumed by users.

To remain compliant, Livingston mentioned a variety of different options companies employ. In some cases, they involve technology. Digital solutions include compliance platforms like Simplify Compliance. Those seeking on the job insights can turn to proven professionals offering up their insights. Consultants, one of the more lucrative positions in and out of the sector, have been brought in to assess organizations as well. Either way, their jobs are to ensure that a company remains on the right side of the ever-changing law.

Other options exist as well. Compliance classes have begun to pop up—providing a career opportunity out of a gap in the sector. In these classes, businesses can begin to better understand laws on the federal, state, and city level. These classes often delve into a number of subjects, including:

- Regulations
- Auditing
- Risk management

- Law
- Standards and practices
- Strategy
- Policy

With compliance essential to a company staying active and open, it should come as little surprise that it represents two of the most in-demand careers in the industry. A survey of 1,200 companies by cannabis career platform Vangst revealed that director of cultivation, who oversees growing, production, and compliance, is one of the hottest jobs in the industry. Second was a compliance manager.

Robert Half Legal's 2019 salary guide delved into the law profession, not cannabis in particular. Despite covering more than marijuana, its information can shed light onto the sector with some margin of error factored in. As with other types of work in the industry, we can look to tangential industries to understand the cannabis law space.

In this case, 85 percent of lawyers surveyed reported having challenges within their organization finding skilled legal professionals for their firm. As such, the report notes that "Employers are competing in a fierce hiring market today." The advantage for job seekers leaves professionals in a favorable position. "Skilled legal professionals are in short supply, and top candidates frequently field multiple job offers. For many roles, the talent crisis is expected to deepen."

The demand for skilled legal talent is known in the space, where talent push for the best compensation packages possible. Robert Half Legal reported, "In addition to a competitive salary, legal job candidates seek comprehensive benefits, flexible hours, an easy commute and work-from-home options, a defined career path and professional development opportunities."

The report listed five in-demand backgrounds to help job seekers:

- Financial Services
- Healthcare and Pharmaceuticals
- Manufacturing
- Professional Services
- Technology

The demand for tech-savvy legal support staff is there as well. The report cited a Bureau of Labor Statistics projection of 15 percent job growth over the next decade for paralegals and legal assistants. Outsourced legal work is in demand as well. Of the more than 200 lawyers surveyed, litigation support, legal research, document review, and contracts were the four most likely tasks to be outsourced to attorneys on a project or contract basis. With law accepting the future of work mentality, freelance law professionals may find an uptick in opportunities in the years ahead.

It should be noted that salaries in the field can vary significantly. Lawyers alone can either earn millions or barely make ends meet depending on their area of work and success.

Outside of law, data from Glassdoor.com revealed that a lobbyist's annual salary can fluctuate quite a bit as well. Location and the company will play a part, just as any sector. A monthly contract for a lobbyist can earn a person $7,000 to $8,000 monthly. A lobbyist at the University of Kansas, or the American Cancer Society, could make anywhere between $42,000 and $52,000 annually. Comparatively, a lobbyist with Lewis-Burke

Associates could bring in an annual revenue between $62,000 and $104,000.

Vangst found that a low skilled compliance manager or a director of cultivation with minimal experience could earn a yearly salary in the mid to upper $40,000 range. A highly qualified person can make upwards of $250,000 per year. on the other end, a minimally experienced compliance manager can earn $45,000 while a highly skilled compliance professional could bring home $149,000.

Salary data from Robert Half Legal showed that lawyers with ten years or more experience can earn between $107,250 to $223,750 or more. A highly skilled general counsel can make over $300,000, while a paralegal manager can earn over $105,000. Most roles do provide livable incomes, even at the early stages; though general administrative work can be on the lower $30,000 range to start.

With such a broad field to work with, compliance careers allow for a number of skilled workers to enter the cannabis space. Livingston mentioned an array of cannabis compliance sectors, including retail management, industrial hygienists, and fire safety engineers as some options. "Cannabis is one of those unique industries that touches everything from agricultural practices and pesticide application to retail sales to dealing with medical information," he pointed out.

On the policy side, he explained that avenues of entry depend on how involved a person wants to be. This applies to whether they prefer business or activism. From there, Livingston suggests finding legitimate groups working on the issue. In cannabis, he noted groups like the Marijuana Policy Project or the Drug Policy Alliance. From there, book meetings with local legislators and state officials. "Those are the people that can really be the most effective in lobbying."

Leland Radovanovic is the Senior Communications Associate at Powerplant Global Strategies. He began his cannabis career when he was eighteen. It was then that he realized cannabis propaganda was just that. From there, he was inspired to make a difference. The first step was moving to New York City and forming a chapter of Students for Sensible Drug Policy. Today, SSDP is the largest international student-led 501c3 non-profit aimed at ending the War on Drugs. "Colorado had just passed its adult use in 2012—I saw the opportunity to help build that momentum for social change. As an advocate, I worked on the passing of New York's medical marijuana laws in 2014."

Two years later, Radovanovic joined the board of another 501c3 non-profit, the Cannabis Cultural Association, which aims to help marginalized and underrepresented communities engage in the cannabis industry while emphasizing criminal justice reform.

Others, like Leo Bridgewater, got involved in cannabis policy reform after experiencing the pains of post-war PTSD, including numerous suicides and even more attempts by close friends. He began working in a New Jersey dispensary and enrolled in the state's medical program in 2015. One night, he talked a friend down from ending their life. It was then that he found out that PTSD was not on the state's qualifying conditions list. This began Bridgewater's quest to make a change. "Rather than continue to keep asking for permissions [to get PTSD added], I just did it."

Since then, he has helped get PTSD added to the qualifying conditions list and remained active in New Jersey's recreational cannabis law provisions, including minority and women ownership as well as criminal justice reform. Today, he continues to advance New Jersey's laws as well as other states striving for similar outcomes.

Those seeking a profession in lobbying can come from all walks of life. As the Princeton Review notes, "Lobbying is a profession full of people who have changed careers, since relevant knowledge and experience are all you really need to become a lobbyist." It added that a college degree is likely, though. "A major in political science, journalism, law, communications, public relations, or economics should stand future lobbyists in good stead. While you're still in college you can check out the terrain through various government-related internships as a congressional aide, in a government agency, or with a lobbying firm, for example."

With such activity on three levels of law, the pressing topics in the space could be a book in its own right.

However, the most talked about topic of 2018, and early 2019, may be the Farm Bill. The bill exempts hemp from the US controlled substances list and provides protections to cultivators. Livingston explained that a good deal of hot topics have to do with the bill to some extent. He pointed out that a lot of compliance is involved, and boils down to what is and isn't legal to label hemp CBD.

In another realm of the sector, shifting policy can upend progress at any time. This is something ABS Engineering and its clients keep in mind when designing their plans. It should be noted that conflicts do arise. As Barkovitz explained, "Generally it's always a struggle between the budget and a client's desires for their facilities/buildout. Most anything is possible with a large budget and an extended timeline, but that is rarely the reality of a project."

Bridgewater's efforts shine a light on discussions on the state level. In New Jersey, Bridgewater said that the issue is battled between progressives, whom he called the Jetsons, and the anti-cannabis lawmakers, labeled as the Flintstones. "To be caught up between two powerhouse egos is an interesting time."

With the bill making progress, Bridgewater and other advocates remain dug in on changing its regulations. A major sticking point has been automatic expungement of certain cannabis-related offenses, which covered an ounce or less at the time of our interview. He explained the importance of this parameter and why he fights for its change.

"What you're saying to me is that you're gonna keep the guy who looks like me in jail for moving a lot of weight back in the day, making hundreds of thousands of dollars, and keep him locked up. Then you're going to bring the guy who doesn't look like me into my neighborhood to move hundreds of pounds of weight and make millions of dollars. That's a problem."

Andrew Livingston helps shape policy as well. In his case, it is through Via Strategies, the government policy wing of his company. There, the economist and regulatory expert gets to be a policy wonk. "Through my time at the law firm and through Via Strategies, I've helped to give tours of cannabis facilities and explain the dynamics of cannabis regulation to public officials in probably over a dozen different countries, as well as many different states. Pretty much every state that has considered cannabis in one form or another."

Correcting cannabis's inclusion and diversity access issues is a concern in the industry. In New Jersey, its proposed bill includes a quota that requires at least 25 percent of businesses are owned by women, minorities, or veterans. Bridgewater was one of the many activists to help influence raise that quota on a previous draft of the bill from 15 to 25 percent.

As cannabis favorability grows, so does the support of law-makers. "The equity issue in cannabis is becoming increasingly high profile as state legislatures are looking to adopt legalization," Livingston explained. "Those state legislators are interested in and really want to ensure that the industry does work to employ people from various, different backgrounds and different races, as well as those businesses, are owned and operated [by them]."

As the industry matures, these policymakers, compliance professionals, and activists will all have a hand in shaping how it operates. For Radovanovic, getting to do so in the non-profit and communications sector has been a fantastic experience. "It's not often you get to choose a career where you are making such a tremendous social and economic impact not only here in the US but globally as well."

The future of each component of the sector looks bright in terms of opportunity. Policy will continue to form on all levels of government. With federal legalization looming, its presence alone fuels so much of the sector.

As policy regulations shift, the need for compliance will only escalate in the years ahead. Brian Barkovitz forecasted where his area of cannabis compliance will go. "National building code organizations like ASHRAE [American Society of Heating, Refrigerating and Air-Conditioning Engineers] are going to form code committees to develop standards that will then be incorporated into state and local codes."

Over time, he sees regulations and compliance becoming more uniform. "There's little consensus around each state, and of course around the country, so it will become a bit more stan-dardized what's required for ventilation, fire protection, energy code, etc."

The marijuana lobby will likely continue to grow as the industry does. Barring any regulation, like it or not, lawmaking and lobbying go hand in hand. At the same time, activists on all sides of the argument will continue to push for legislation and regulations.

As such, some careers in the sector can earn a person thousands—or even millions. Others will more likely earn more rewards through their achievements rather than salary. Regardless of the path, the ability to shape how legal cannabis looks in the years ahead is immensely worthwhile.

11

Creative, PR, Branding, and Marketing

Cannabis branding, public relations, and marketing are essential to a brand's growth. With federal regulations limiting advertising on social media and other popular methods like Google AdWords, creative PR and marketing are essential. Whether dedicated solely to cannabis or just part of its portfolio, both in-house teams, agencies, and single-person ventures are helping get the word out about cannabis.

This wasn't the case even just a few years ago; it was quite common to find one person holding numerous roles, doing their best to market and brand their company. Now, with revenues increasing, there is a rising need for numerous roles, including:

- Copywriters
- Content Producers
- Social Media Managers
- UX Designers
- Graphic Designers
- Digital Strategists

These roles are in demand with companies in legal markets, as well as on the illicit market where products and services currently operate while waiting for legalization to come one day. This is also the case with grey market, where illicit products look and resemble products from a legal, state-approved source.

More experienced professionals are also in demand, with director and management positions needed in each function. These roles are attracting top names outside of cannabis as well. Last fall, cannabis operator Cresco Labs made a splash by hiring ex-Nike Global Creative Director Scott Wilson. Around the time of the news, he explained to *Forbes* that, "For me it's working with like-minded entrepreneurs and clients and pioneering new territories."

As in any case, salaries can vary depending on the company and the work arrangement; often these roles can be outsourced to freelance workers or digital agencies. That said, full-time salaried positions are quite common as well—and most positions pay a livable to significant wage depending on experience.

Global Human Resources consulting firm Robert Half's 2019 Creative & Marketing Salary Guide, which was conducted by its creative staffing firm The Creative Group, found that even new and still developing professionals could often earn upwards of $50,000 or more per year. Some roles include copywriter ($58,250), video editor ($53,250), interaction designer ($64,500), and graphic designer ($42,000). At their most skilled, managers and executives often earned near or over $100,000.

That said, not all career options in the market can be viable. Roles like entry-level production assistants ($31,750), production coordinators ($37,500), and traffic coordinators ($33,750) were career paths that paid even its most skilled just over $62,000 annually. This type of pay can make working in cities and major metropolitan areas difficult to live on.

The Creative Group's report also found a wide variety of salaries depending on a person's location. Factors including cost of living and scarcity of talent played into the fluctuating numbers. In all, the report found that locations like New York City, Washington, D.C., and Los Angeles saw the average salary of professionals increase 40.5 percent, 33 percent, and 32 percent, respectively. Meanwhile, professionals in markets such as El Paso (TX), Duluth (MN), and Canton (OH) saw its average salary decline by 28 percent, 20.4 percent, and 18 percent.

Meanwhile, one standout in Virginia, Tysons Corner, saw its average salary rise 32 percent above the national average.

With that in mind, aspiring professionals can find numerous ways to get into the market. Some have found success directly out of college while others found themselves in the field after they weren't fulfilled in their previous sector.

Heather Carter, Director of Communications for REVEL,

New York City's cannabis innovation and networking event group, made the jump after not finding fulfillment doing similar work in the pharma space. In fact, her emergence in cannabis came after a layoff from PR work.

"When I first entered into this space I was scared to promote myself because it had been a while since I [had] done any PR and social media marketing. However, people needed those services. So, I had to hold my head high, step up to the plate, and handle my business." She explained how she overcame the negatives of her last PR role to excel in cannabis. "My last PR job made me feel as if I was incapable of doing PR work, but I had to reflect on my past experiences and accomplishments and realize that I could do it. Being afraid to fail was my biggest fear, but I took a chance on myself and I'm so glad that I did."

Others make the jump from working in other facets of cannabis. For example, Leland Radovanovic's journey to PR was detailed in the chapter on policymaking.

Then there are people like Cain Castor, who made his opportunity out of hardship. After graduating from Penn State with a finance degree in 2017, Castor joined a Fortune 500 tech company, only to be laid off the following year during a 40 percent company downsizing. He used the time off to refocus his career. "For the next few months, I started redefining my skill, and finding out exactly what services I could offer. I had a number of skills from photoshop and graphic design to creating marketing strategies."

This led to working in the electronic dance music space, where he and some colleagues oversaw the design and print roll campaign for the duo DVBBS. After turning away from EDM, the group focused on cannabis and its better opportunities. In September 2018, he landed a Branding Coordinator role with Origin House, formerly CannaRoyalty. Castor's time there proved invaluable. He claims that working with a team across seven brands helped him better understand the retail space while working on a number of marketing campaigns and brand strategies. Since then, Castor helped re-launch the group's digital agency, Good People, before pivoting back to contract marketing.

For Carter, her switch to cannabis was one filled with passion, something she believes can take her further than money. This passion allows her to push herself in an uncharted industry. "You have to be willing to go above and beyond what your 'job duty' is because this is such a new industry and we're the ones setting the groundwork/creating the framework for what is going to stand many decades from now." She explains that "I don't know" isn't an acceptable answer.

While the stance may seem cold, it is actually how the field operates today. With little time to waste, answers have to be found, ideally in short order. For Carter and other proponents of cannabis ethos, it comes back to community. "You have to find a way to know. Go into your rolodex and see how other industry partners and insiders can advise you until you find the answer you're looking for. We aren't in competition with each other. We're building together."

Meanwhile, Radovanovic has learned how to make real change by understanding people, their values, and speaking to their concerns. He has also understood that his work is a hurry-up-and-wait environment that hinges on the schedules of clients and the media. "Often, we need to make an announcement for a company in the next 24 hours, just to have it delayed due to things outside our control. Or, we get the announcement out, and that reporter has written on it recently, they are away on vacation, or like many others have hundreds of emails to sift through a day to find the most interesting news in the coverage area."

For Castor, his journey has taught him the value of flexibility. "If you come from a rigid corporate structure, cannabis will be hard to get a grasp of. If you can get a feel for the constant changes, and develop the ability to pivot in any direction necessary, you will have a much easier time."

The learning never stops for professionals in the evolving cannabis space. Radovanovic explained how communications professionals are often discussing how to segment different audiences. At the same time, using new language to demonstrate the safety of cannabis as a medicine has been a frequent topic of discussion.

Overall, professionals in the creative and marketing spaces note a wealth of benefits —specifically working in a new industry with a tight-knit group of people who are changing the conversation around cannabis. That said, the industry—like any other—has its drawbacks.

For PR and media professionals, the influx of news can be staggering to even seasoned veterans. Radovanovic explained that, "The rate of news and content creation is blistering, and catching not only reporters' attention but also the attention of the public is difficult. For every one journalist, there are six of me vying for their attention."

Both Carter and Castor noted how the industry is subject to scores of trial and error. Positives can be found when errors occur. As Castor explained, "Most executive teams are open to trying out new, outside-the-box marketing tactics because there's no perfect formula . . . yet." He added that this type of arrangement could be beneficial to professionals coming from other industries. "Your direct output will help shape the market. If you are coming from an outside industry, you can use your expertise to help shape the current market."

One of the more pressing issues surrounds branding. Trademark Attorney Amanda Osorio explained that "The US Patent and Trademark Office [USPTO] does not allow trademark registrations for illegal substances or any paraphernalia related to illegal substances or illegal services. For the cannabis industry, any claimed products or services that would violate the federal Controlled Substances Act will cause the application to be refused registration." Osorio noted how this impacts cannabis companies branding in the US as well. "Even major brands in the cannabis space have been unable to obtain federal trademark registrations and therefore trademark protection under the federal laws in the US." Even with those hurdles, Osorio pointed out that some brands have been able to register marks for t-shirts or other items that they also sell.

Another aspect of branding that limits cannabis is marketing. Companies often rely on social media and Google ads to build their brands. That is also not allowed due to the regulations on cannabis. While some have bemoaned about the issue, others see no problem with it. Kris Lenz, Content Marketing Manager for MGO|ELLO National Cannabis Alliance, a CPA and professional services firm, is one of the latter.

"Anyone hemming and hawing over advertising rules and restrictions has never worked in a highly regulated industry before," Lenz explained. "Cannabis is an intoxicating substance and it is only natural, and right, to have rules around where, when, and how cannabis advertising operates. Alcohol and tobacco have been navigating similar sets of rules for a long time."

Instead of strict regulations, Lenz pointed toward another issue. "The only real issue here is that marketers are not likely to be up-to-date on the rules and are making mistakes. But with time and experience, that will change."

Another glaring downside of the industry is one that runs across cannabis and every other major market: diversity. While Carter gave credit to women of color in the communications and marketing space—including Dasheeda Dawson of MJM Strategy, Gia Moran of GVM Communications, and Tracey Henry of Tracey Henry Consulting (THC)—she noted a lack of diversity in the sector. Radovanovic echoed these sentiments. "There are amazing companies currently run by women and women of color," before adding, "not enough sit on our haunches and be proud about."

Castor shared similar feelings across employees, leadership, and ownership. "The workforce is more diverse, with much more representation of women and minorities, but is still majority white and male. However, cannabis is taking a step in the right direction with more female leadership than most other sectors."

Plenty of states and cannabis companies are seeking a diverse and talented staff. The Creative Group 2019 report found that some of the top skills employers seek include AI and machine learning, content creation, digital strategy, SEO/SEM and video production to name a few.

Of the six hundred creative and marketing professionals polled, 71 percent reported a difficulty finding talent with the up-to-date digital skills the company required. This, however, could be a problem residing within companies. The Creative Group explained that this perfect hire may not actually exist. Instead, it suggests that companies find adequate talent and train them with additional skills.

Radovanovic noted that PR firms seek out professionals who require little oversight and can meet tight deadlines. "Thinking strategically requires thoughtfulness, which is difficult when are you moving at lightspeed, so being able to stay calm and cool under immense pressure is an absolute must."

Radovanovic noted that applicants should be able to show quantifiable results like growing brands in new markets and enhancing revenue. "The large cannabis companies will continue to grow and will look to the mainstream to take top talent, so you have to get in now and make a splash."

In addition to these traits, an ideal professional in the PR space should be on top of the news so that they can develop a deep knowledge of the industry. Those like REVEL's Carter explain that a passion for the plant is often part of the hiring process. So, it may be best to know the plant before applying.

Castor's previous firm sought applicants who demonstrated a flexible temperament with creative and organizational skills to boot. He also mentions understanding the industry, a classic point people tend to forget (whether they are in cannabis or elsewhere). Lastly, he says be ready to make a mark on the company and industry. "Cannabis is a feast or famine market."

So far, the professionals who spoke with me regard their experience fondly for the most part. While calling his experience "one hell of a rollercoaster," Castor also added, "I've been able to accomplish more in cannabis than in any other market in the past." Meanwhile, Carter has learned and made lots of valuable connections. "I am very fortunate to have met the people I've met in this industry and to have my partners at REVEL."

The future of the cannabis industry appears bright. As such, Radovanovic believes that extends to the work done by professionals in the fields discussed in this chapter. "Communications and PR will continue to grow as the cannabis industry develops. Our job has never been more important—shaping an emerging industry with immense implications to our economy and its social impact."

However, questions do linger. Osorio noted how trademarks could become an intriguing subject if cannabis is permitted for adult use. "It will be interesting to see what happens if the federal government legalizes marijuana because I anticipate that there will be a lot of interest in filing federal trademark registration applications, as well as an uptick in trademark infringement litigation between companies in the cannabis industry."

With such excitement and intrigue, this large sector offers ample opportunity for job seekers. Those able to weather the volatility of the sector could find themselves in a position growing some of the first wave of mega players in cannabis. While pain points are evident, so is the excitement and possibility that comes with crafting creative solutions.

12

Experiences, Events, and Entertainment

An in-person experience can create an immense impact on an individual. Per Alon Alroy, co-founder and Chief of Customer Success for Bizzabo Co, "Ninety-five percent of marketers believe that in-person events provide attendees with a valuable opportunity to form connections in an increasingly digital world." As such, the world of experiences, events, and entertainment is invaluable to today's burgeoning cannabis scene.

Alroy added that this sector should only expand in the coming years. "As the events industry continues to grow, we predict cannabis events will follow suit. Over the years, we've seen increasing amounts of cannabis-related events arrive on the scene, some of which have become our partners. The landscape is still somewhat fragmented, with smaller events making up the majority."

He explained how the industry could benefit from the continued progress. "If the process of legalization continues, cannabis events will benefit from additional sponsorship opportunities, larger budgets, and greater brand recognition. All of the above will contribute to cannabis conferences that are grander in scale and the emergence of smaller roadshow events that are able to bring relevant content to attendees wherever they may be."

David Hua, founder and CEO of dispensary point-of-sale technology Meadow, talked about some of the events his company has helped power in recent memory, including the 2018 Emerald Cup. "These types of experiences where you can meet the farmers and enjoy sampling different strains is something we're going to see more of as California cities begin to solidify their approach to hosting cannabis events. People want to know more about cannabis, where it comes from, and how to enjoy it responsibly." Going forward, he is excited for the day when cannabis consumption lounges are the norm at major festivals and events.

Today, the sector already offers a variety of cannabis events—from pop ups to experiential marketing to music festivals to meetups with vendors selling their finest flower and other goodies. With such a wide offering of career opportunities, numerous types of people and backgrounds have found their way into the market.

Ellen Hancock was born in cannabis country in Northern California, but didn't get involved in the industry right away. "I sort of grew up in the black-market cannabis industry, but then left that behind and followed a career in modeling and acting. However, when the dust kind of settled after legalization, and cannabis business started to seem safe and legitimate in California, I knew I wanted to get involved again." Today, the actor, model, and improviser is active as the "Stoner Girlfriend," a cannabis advocate, brand ambassador, and on-camera host.

Hancock is now based in Los Angeles where she reaps the benefits of being in the thick of media and advertising. "I'm finding that my skills in front of the camera and with public speaking and networking are pretty niche when you also add in my knowledge and experience within the cannabis industry. So I'm finding a lot of opportunity with brands and media outlets to sort of be a face and voice for their marketing initiatives, as well as helping connect them to other strategic partners."

On the other end is Sasha Perelman, who is in her third year as an entrepreneur. Perelman moved to Los Angeles from New York and has since launched Revolver Productions, a full-service event management and experiential agency. She also started Mary Talks, a cannabis event series which has held events in major cannabis markets, medicinal and adult use, including Los Angeles, New York City, and Seattle. Event themes have included cannabis and culinary, as well as pot and performance. "My goal through experiential events and my recent project, Mary Talks, is to educate the masses on cannabis as a wellness and lifestyle tool. People can heal themselves with plant medicine and use it as an alternative to opioids and other toxic treatments."

It would be remiss to not acknowledge the events happening on the illicit market as well. They include cannabis showcases tucked away in discreet locations, from homes to nightclubs. Here, events are often put on with the same professional caliber one may find in California, except they happen to be held in a market that doesn't have adult-use legislation on the books. Guests can find a range of offerings at such events, like complimentary dabs, CBD-infused mocktails, and infused food made by some of the top chefs in the culinary space.

"Sidney" is an events producer in both legal and illicit markets across the US. They noted how cities like New York City have shifted to a grey market in recent years. As such, there's been an inundation of cannabis events. They described how one culinary events producer is going beyond food to provide guests with memorable experiences. "They're incorporating a spiritual aspect to it that isn't just about flavor and consumption." They also expect that more events should come soon enough. "For the most part, I think we're all going to take a year to flagrantly consume massive amounts of cannabis before we start getting into what creative consumption looks like," they explained.

Speaking of culinary events, getting into the field comes via numerous access points. Some chefs come with culinary backgrounds while others found their way into a career after discovering their passion and talent for infused cooking and baking. While some have turned their passion into a profession, others are straddling the line in other professions while the market heats up.

The diverse options in the sector allow for a professional to find their footing in a number of markets. Hancock noted the benefits of her current home. "Los Angeles is huge in the industry right now with the Silicon Beach startup vibe, events and celebrity-owned brands, links to media and entertainment, and its close proximity and free access to some of the best marijuana growing regions in the country."

For those seeking a market ripe for the picking, she noted two East Coast areas. "On the flip side, if you want to get in on the ground floor somewhere—I'd start making plans in New York or Miami. They are just starting to get the buzz of business, and once they legalize in the coming years . . . it would pay to already be a familiar voice in the movement."

New York City and Los Angeles are major media markets and are readily embracing events both legal and illicit. Marketers have embraced experiential cannabis events on the most mainstream of levels. That includes HBO, who is no stranger to cannabis. One of its shows, *High Maintenance*, deals with pot delivery in New York City. To promote its third season, HBO teamed up with experiential company Grandesign to serve up free CBD lattes to people in Brooklyn and Venice Beach.

Traditional advertising and marketing is in the mix as well. In February 2019, retailer MedMen launched an ad campaign which detailed the history of cannabis in America from the counterculture to becoming part of the country's culture. The spot featured actor and activist Jesse Williams, and was directed by Academy Award–winning filmmaker Spike Jonze. Though, the TV show *South Park* may have made the ad even more popular when it spoofed the spot on its episode Tegridy Farms."

One of the entertainment community's biggest nights also turned to cannabis. For the 2019 Oscar Awards, nominees and attendees found some new items in their swag bags. Guests were given VIP memberships to MOTA, a cannabis-friendly social club as well as cannabis-infused edibles and topicals.

High-end brands are getting involved as well. Sidney described how this incorporation of retail and cannabis may look. "I think when you start thinking about like Barneys opening up dispensaries in Los Angeles, and you start seeing high,

high end retail, or like high fashion capital, getting involved in cannabis in Manhattan, it's not just going to be retail. A lot of that is going to be experience based. Because if I am going to a Chanel dispensary, or I'm going to a Barneys dispensary, is an eighth going to be $20 because we know the actual price of the flower, or is it going to be $200 because it's like a full premium product? Or, is the eighth going to be free or is that all going to just be complimentary? And then what you're selling is this clubhouse, this bourgeoisie clubhouse consumptive experience."

Celebrities are getting more and more involved in the business. Snoop Dogg and Willie Nelson are now bona fide cannabis leaders, expanding from their days of pro-cannabis music and acting to heading up their own ventures. Today, other names are taking sizable steps into entertainment as well. Former World Heavyweight boxing champ Mike Tyson is one of them. In February 2019, he held a cannabis-friendly pop-up music festival at his Tyson Ranch in Desert Hot Springs, Arizona. In addition to holding concerts, Tyson's 412-acre resort also boasts a cannabis research facility.

As Bizzabo and Alroy noted, cannabis events are on the rise. They include mainstays like MJBizCon, with its marquee event held in Las Vegas, as well as the National Cannabis Industry Association's Seed to Sale Cannabis Conference in Boston. Scores of others are hitting not-yet-legal markets while also tapping into niche sectors that hold ample amounts of opportunity. They include the Brooklyn Cannabis Expo, which will feature two days of typical event fare, including panels, discussions, and entertainment.

Others are tapping into specific needs in booming sectors. They include the Cannabis Wedding Expo. In 2016, wedding website The Knot found that the average wedding cost $32,329.

A report from IBISWorld found the overall wedding industry valued at $72 billion. With those numbers, it's no surprise that expos are currently planned for Las Vegas, Los Angeles, San Francisco, and Denver. With legislation easing in other states, more wedding-centric cannabis events could pop up soon enough.

With such an array of services and products, it would be difficult to estimate any average salaries for the sector overall. Instead, we can look to non-cannabis-based roles for an idea. Data from ZipRecruiter.com found that Events Coordinators in Brooklyn earned around $41,000 on average, with top professionals earning upward of $60,000 in the role. The site noted that private chefs in the same city can earn an average of $72,000 per year, while earning in excess of $150,000 for some. On the other hand, most actors earn an average of roughly $28,000 annually.

These figures do shed some light on what a person can earn, but it has to be remembered that this is a burgeoning industry with a significant amount of illicit-market activity. As such, private cannabis chefs in Brooklyn can earn more for high-end events while others struggle to scale up their business. For example, experiential marketing is a lucrative business that doesn't touch the cannabis plant. Making a six-figure salary in this line of work may be more attainable than others. In terms of entertainment, the volatility can never be truly gauged. While some never catch on with paying roles, others excel on a regular, well-paid basis. Keep in mind that hot and cold streaks happen all the time in this line of work and a guaranteed income may not be possible for most, even if they are a well-known name in the space.

Both Perelman and Hancock agree that the cannabis industry

as a whole is exciting and rife with opportunity. They also noted how it has its drawbacks. Perelman pointed toward one of California's most frustrating aspects of its market: regulations. She called the laws "ever-changing," which costs owners like her heaps of money to continually stay out of the grey area.

Hancock noted a general lack of organization by many, in addition to "shady players trying to get ahead at any cost." She explained that not everyone is in it for the ethics the cannabis industry embraced decades ago. She pointed out that, "With a lot of the industry still a bit unstable and off the books, there's a lot of ways shitty people are taking advantage of those trying to do legitimate business. I've heard of numerous cases of supposed business partners stealing ideas, merchandise, trademarks. And everyone is trying to lowball everyone else or get work done for free." She noted how many in the industry want to pay in product and not a paycheck. "I find I have to really fight hard for my rates on cannabis-specific gigs, because right now everyone thinks they can just pay you with free product. Free weed doesn't pay bills, people!"

Hancock highlighted other pressing concerns in the space, which include leaders of companies who have allegedly dubious pasts. She also points toward the disproportionate rate that people of color are incarcerated for cannabis crimes, as well as the declining presence of female cannabis executive leadership, a trend in the sector.

Despite the drawbacks, both Perelman and Hancock have enjoyed their cannabis careers thus far. "Working in the cannabis space has helped me align with my greater purpose in the world," said Perelman. "It has expanded my network of friends and collaborators to include some of the most brilliant minds and kind-hearted individuals. There is a real sense of community in the industry. People coming together as change agents to really propel cannabis into the limelight with integrity and vigor."

These roles are just some of what a job seeker or entrepreneur can find in the experiences, events, and entertainment sectors of the industry. Those seeking work may need to tap into their cannabis network—this is especially true in illegal markets where a person's reputation is all that one can rely on. In other cases, where a person isn't touching the plant, marketers and event producers could find work making inroads as any other professional in the space. The same can be said for entertainers, brand ambassadors, and a number of others delving into entertainment and user-generated content marketing or advertising. People can also pursue their own ventures. They include legal experiences—like Perelman's work—or they could be under the radar while regulation reform awaits in certain major markets.

With such a wide variety of options and an even broader base of pay, this is a line of work that may not be suited for everyone. Those seeking stable pay may only be able to explore a sliver of the sector. If one is open to fluctuating pay, customer, demand and long hours of work, then this may be the field for them. The opportunity is already there, and will only expand.

David Hua pointed out how a person can stand out. "It's a nuanced space. The more familiarity people have with cannabis in general, the better equipped they are to operate in this complex industry. Ideally, people should have familiarity with the different types of industry events that already exist, the regulatory landscape, and an understanding of cannabis brands and products to better find strategic partners to help create experiences at events."

13

Freelance

Some call it freelancing. Others refer to it as the gig economy. Whatever the case may be, independent contractors can make a living in the cannabis industry just as they've proven to do so in other markets. The 2018 Freelancing in America report from gig economy platform Upwork and the Freelancer's Union found that 56.7 million Americans participated in the freelance workforce. This represented a 3.7 million gain from 2014. Of those polled, 77 percent reported that freelance provided them with an improved work/life balance. Forty-two percent claimed that freelance work provided them with the flexibility they could not find in traditional employment.

Data released in the summer of 2018 from the Bureau of Labor Statistics found that independent contractors—including consultants and freelancers—is the largest work arrangement outside of the traditional office. The report noted 10.6 million independent contractors working in America as of May 2017. Interestingly, the report also stated that one in three of those in the workforce were aged fifty-five or older.

The BLS findings also reported that two-thirds of the workforce were men, and were more often than not white. However, a 2017 survey of the entire gig economy by Hyperwallet did find that an increasing number of women are freelancing, but not in a full-time capacity.

Hyperwallet found that of its 2,000 respondents, 59 percent of female gig workers have spouses with full-time careers who also contribute to the household income. Of those 2,000, 70 percent are the primary caregiver in their homes. Additionally, 61 percent would like to make gig work their full-time career.

Despite the signs of growth in cannabis and the gig economy, the two economists who predicted the industry boom in 2015, Princeton University's Alan Krueger and Harvard's Lawrence Katz, now believe that their study was wrong. Krueger recently told the *Wall Street Journal* that "Larry Katz and I now conclude that there was a modest rise in the share of the workforce in nontraditional jobs over the last decade—probably on the order of one to two percentage points, instead of the five percentage point rise we originally reported."

While the status of the gig economy as a whole remains up for debate, the state of the cannabis industry's freelance market is that much more in flux. A lack of industry-specific data leaves those searching for answers to parse through information and the anecdotes of those in the space.

The need for freelancers in cannabis is on the rise. Depending on the service provided, freelancers can find a wealth of opportunity or may have to be one of the early trailblazers in the space.

Freelancers can find work in a number of ways; one that many turn to are traditional job search platforms. From LinkedIn to Indeed.com to a plethora of others, freelance work certainly can be found on these sites. Some were better than others at helping produce worthwhile results—though nothing catered explicitly to the cannabis market.

But in 2018, that began to change. Denise Biderman and Taylor Aldredge got to work on the first cannabis-specific freelance job board, Mary's List. Their work garnered the attention of Boston University's Innovate@BU Start-up Competition—which awarded them a $10,000 prize in November 2018. The platform launched a few months later, and has begun to see modest gains recruiting freelancers and notable clients.

Mary's List intends to provide freelancers in the cannabis industry with their first dedicated platform, while also providing workers with data they sorely lack at this time. Aldredge explained that freelancers may be in the dark for a few more years. "My goal in the future would be that we could be the source of all that information, but we're years away from even knowing what works like that."

One thing that Aldredge has noted is that freelancers are often not working solely in cannabis; other work is needed to sustain their living. "It's very rare that one of our people only does cannabis stuff. They're building a brand around it...they have, for example, wedding photographers where they have an art service they do, but then they also do wedding photography."

The site offers sectors from accounting to catering to customer service. However, it will need to scale up its users and companies if it wants to sustain. While the company notes modest gains each day in users, finding companies can be more difficult. To garner attention, the company has relied on content and inbound marketing to educate their audience.

In the first few months of operation, registering users and job leads have trickled in. With market awareness a key factor in its longevity, Mary's List finds itself like plenty in the cannabis space: a useful platform with potential, if the market uses it. As of August 2019, the site had minimal job postings but did remain active in sharing listings on social media.

Vangst recently entered into the freelance market as well. In the summer of 2018, it launched an offshoot of its original platform, Vangst Gigs, which is geared toward freelancers. The freelance hub touts working with notable cannabis brands like PAX, Harborside, Native Roots, Baker, and others. So far, however, the work is limited to roles in trimming, budtending, packaging, and post-harvesting.

Aldredge noted other freelance sectors that have become more in demand, noting a significant need for sales and business development professionals. Creatives such as writers and graphic designers are also in demand. Aldredge noted a particular need for designers. He explained that, "everybody needs some sort of graphics work, whether it's for a website or print or anything else design-wise." Consultants also received significant recognition. Aldredge noted that consultants are vital to the development of large projects and are needed in a variety of cannabis projects.

He noted that application writing may be the most necessary service at this time. "The biggest opportunity in my mind is application writing, permit applications, like any of that stuff because that's where most of the states are. They're getting licenses out. They're trying to get people to have their standard operating procedures or their education books and all that stuff that they're writing. There's so much writing help needed. Whether it's legal, online, copy, it's just a lot of setup right now."

Despite noting certain markets, Aldredge was quick to point out that nothing should be off-limits for freelancers. If a company realizes it could save money by outsourcing aspects of its operations, then they may consider hiring a freelancer.

Finding freelance cannabis jobs on numerous platforms produced little results outside of a few sectors. A few postings (listed few and far between) show that there have been needs for sales, creative, and e-commerce work. The startup platform AngelList generated slightly more results than most boards, though the amount was still underwhelming. In the past few months, cannabis companies that address customer engagement, telemedicine, and compliance were some of the nine startups offering contract roles, including inside sales rep, brand ambassador, and on-screen personalities.

Some in-demand roles may not be considered freelance for much longer—that includes delivery drivers. In the fall of 2018, the state of California found that these drivers were not independent contractors and rather employees of the company.

Concerning income, freelancers can find their pay varying depending on several factors. In cannabis and beyond, many independent contractors are hesitant of job bidding sites. These platforms are often regarded as sources of cheap or free work. In some cases, only people living internationally with significantly lower costs of living can feasibly accept such roles.

A search of cannabis freelancers on Upwork revealed a mixed bag of rates. Some working in management and business planning were charging $60/hour. Other consultants offered $30/hour. Writers tended to vary between $25 and $75/hour. Others in marketing charged around $75/hour.

That said, it is not known how often these proposed rates are accepted on sites like Upwork. A race to the bottom is often a problem on those platforms. In these cases, the client often only wants the lowest-priced worker. Additionally, the saturation of applicants can prove to be a dangerous combination to job seekers. Though some North American independent contractors have found success and consistent work on these platforms, scores of others dismiss them for their lack of payoff, both literally and metaphorically. However, those in emerging countries, or others able to live off tight earnings, could find paydays and resume boosts as well.

Looking at the above findings, one may assume that now is not the ideal time to get into freelance cannabis work. That may be true for some sectors but it does not seem to be the case. There exists an ample amount of opportunity for the taking at this time. Going beyond job boards, freelancers can find themselves with a wealth of opportunity by taking the job sourcing into their own hands. Though, they must apply themselves or see the market grow without them involved.

Freelancers can succeed by putting themselves out there both online and in person. The key is to become involved. Cannabis has always been a community, and is now expanding to become one with a vibrant business culture and people. Freelancers can benefit from this by adopting client sourcing practices from other sectors to their work in cannabis. The tried and true methods of networking and cold outreach are both viable avenues for independent job seekers. Maintaining an online brand via social media, a personal website, and a portfolio website are ideal for attracting inbound traffic. You can set up a portfolio in a number of ways. Designers can use sites like Behance, Adobe, Wix, or others. Writers may find luck on Contently or Muck Rack. Both of these professionals and many others also can find success by creating their own website on sites like Squarespace as well.

Most of the current cannabis industry will say that networking is the prime way one can find clients in the space. This is a rule that has applied to countless industries throughout time. Its importance in cannabis is much more essential at this time. With the market just developing, entrepreneurs are cautious of who they work with. With such a demand for growth and little time to vet an employee, people in the cannabis community turn to their networks for recommendations. As such, face-to-face meetings are vital; making the right impressions on influential people is how you find work. Once in the mix with these people, you can expect more opportunities that they connect you with. The more time in the sector, the more people you meet. And with everyone working together, sharing information, having positive contacts will keep you working.

By networking, you have the opportunity to meet the influential figures in the space. You'll also come across scores of tables presenting their products, services, and causes. Stop at each table and learn about what is being offered. Often, these bootstrapped companies don't have the budget to send team members to the events. This offers you the rare opportunity to immediately attract the attention of a company's founder, CEO, or other influential decision makers.

Depending on the client, your skill may not be enough. While some companies tend to care less about cannabis ethos—a concern shared among plenty in the space—others are founded upon them. For them, it takes a combination of know-how and passion.

Aldredge noted this passion among most of cannabis's freelancers. "[Ideal job seekers] have a general passion for this plant that goes beyond just making money. They want to help people find medicine, helping them feel better."

Jyl Ferris is a long-time independent worker through her cannabis marketing venture, Jyl Ferris Design. She has found video, web, and print work with clients such as Tikun Olam, as well as major names outside of cannabis like *Vogue*, the NBA, and *Harper's Bazaar* to name a few. She credits the networking community in New York City for getting her into the industry. Her efforts to be a valuable member of the community certainly helped her get noticed.

"I found the New York groups—High NY and Women Grow. CannaGather came a little later, but close behind." She explained what she did to give to the community and show her value. "I started volunteering at Women Grow. I wanted to show who I was. I wanted to show that I'm capable, that I'm active, that I know my stuff." She also found value in the materials being presented at these events. "I also felt that I needed an education beyond my own personal experience with cannabis."

Regardless of the work a freelancer pursues, part of their work will always be sales and marketing if they want to succeed. In addition to job boards and networking, traditional outreach methods are an excellent way to set up calls and book clients. Like networking, cold outreach allows you to network with the industry by presenting your work and how it can be a solution to a client's needs.

When I started working as a freelance cannabis writer, I relied on my experience working in business development for startups. To establish my targets, I searched job boards, AngelList, numerous cannabis company listing pages, LinkedIn, and good ol' fashion Google searches to find the sectors I knew and cared about the most.

From there, I would source email contact info and draft up an email offering my services and a chance to speak over the phone. Each email followed a loose template that quickly established my interest and knowledge in the company while noting how I could be of service. Next, I'd dive into my experience using only a few sentences. From there, I would include a link to my portfolio and close by asking if we could speak at their convenience.

If you do not receive a response, reach out with a short follow-up in five to seven business days. If they don't answer back, then send one more email the next week acknowledging that now is not the time to speak and leave the door open to reconnect when they are ready. That third email is vital, and sometimes produces clients months down the road. Plus, it can be refreshing to see a past name pop up with your next opportunity.

Freelancers often have the luxury of choosing where to work. The same applies for most freelancers currently working in cannabis. However, one should remember that the market is still emerging. Having a presence in the market may be crucial at this time. So, while working internationally is feasible, it is important to assess how often you may be needed on-site.

That said, both North America and the rest of the world offer freelancers with a wealth of options to choose as their home base.

Nomad List may be one of the most comprehensive analyses of freelance destinations across the globe. The site analyzes common factors such as the cost of living, Internet speed, WiFi availability, and other freelance must-haves. Furthermore, it examines city life from weather to air quality to overall citizen happiness. To round out its scores, the site analyzes the city's freedom of speech and treatment of minorities, women, LGBTQ, and foreigners.

One North American city, Mexico City (Mexico), cracked the top five, which had Canggu Bali (Indonesia), as its top freelancer destination. Not many North American locations came near topping the list. Montreal (Canada) came in 40th, with Puerto Vallarta (Mexico) coming in 43rd. Las Vegas was the first city in the United States to make the list, at 48.

Cannabis freelancers may also want to pause before choosing certain international locations for work. In addition, certain countries remain incredibly anti-cannabis. Your profession could find you having to deal with the authorities, even if you aren't touching the plant. The site does have a premium filter that highlights locations which have decriminalized cannabis, for those interested.

For some, the cost of living is the prime driver in their location. According to 2017 data compiled by HowMuch.net, the cheapest cities for freelancers in the United States were:

1. Spokane, WA: $32,641
2. North Las Vegas, NV: $25,277
3. Las Vegas, NV: $24,917
4. Henderson, NV: $21,193
5. Reno, NV: $20,837
6. Buffalo, NY: $19,786
7. Jacksonville, FL: $18,812
8. Fort Worth, TX: $17,968

9. Laredo, TX: $16,048
10. Newark, NJ: $14,989

HowMuch's research found that only two non-coastal cities were seen as financially out of reach: Austin (Texas) Nashville (Tennessee).

Freelancing, no matter the industry, is an endeavor not made for everyone. As the cannabis industry matures, the current crop of independent contractors serves as the first wave in the field. Additional learning and patience is needed. With such rapid growth and investment comes ample opportunity. Those who have entered this type of work thus far have the first-to-market advantage in establishing their name and reputation in their cannabis sectors.

Each sector of the industry remains ripe for the taking. The key is to find your service, offer a solution, and keep pursuing deals. Be it through job boards, networking, marketing, and/or cold outreach, find the most lucrative pipelines for your business and go from there. The work won't stop, but a solid foundation will have you set up for success as best you can.

Remember that with each job comes an opportunity to shape your reputation in the space. By establishing a track record as a reliable, punctual, and thoughtful collaborator, a job seeker is likely to find themselves at the top of the list of that person's next job. And when they have a colleague in need, guess who they will turn to?

All it takes is sourcing the first few jobs. You never know where it can take you.

14

Entrepreneur

Some reading this book may still not have any inkling of where they fit into the cannabis industry. For others, they may have known all along that no previous chapter truly applied to them. If so, it is likely because they weren't meant to work for anyone but themselves.

Entrepreneurs are represented in all sectors of the workforce. They create the ventures that produce jobs and income for others, as well as tax revenue for the government. Be they company founders or executives or freelancers, each are the leaders of their business—possibly even their industry. With cannabis able to replicate a sector from any other non-cannabis market, ample opportunity awaits those that are able to ride out the highs and lows of an evolving behemoth industry.

With prohibition thawing, the cannabis industry is finally emerging out of the illicit market and stepping into the mainstream. As it creeps out of its long, needless exile, gaping holes riddle each sector. Even if legacy cannabis leaders are there to help steer its growth, no verticals or established brands have been able to emerge until most recently. As such, the need for more products and services is a common occurrence across the industry.

With such an opportunity on the table, entrepreneurs should build from their strengths, explained Harborside's DeAngelo. The Harborside co-founder, activist, and educator explained to me how a person can enter the industry by tapping into what they already know. "If you're a software person, take a look at cannabis software. If you're an agriculture person, look at conservation. If you're a marketer, then start looking at branding."

This is a sentiment shared by entrepreneurs like Ross Lipson, co-founder and CEO of Dutchie, a cannabis delivery service in Oregon. In a February 2019 article for *Green Entrepreneur*, Lipson explained how his strengths from other sectors allowed him to create a delivery and education service for the cannabis space. In the article, Lipson wrote that, "The concept wasn't completely random. In my previous life, I ran and sold two online food-ordering companies. The first I helped start in college after I noticed how much time students wasted looking through stacks of paper menus and calling restaurants for delivery. After graduating, I discovered there were no online food-delivery businesses in Canada, so my partner and I created GrubCanada, scaled it from coast to coast, and sold it to Just Eat in 2012."

The experiences of Lipson and other entrepreneurs prove why it is wise to rely on previous strengths. Cannabis is its own industry and will be enough of a learning curve. It harbors thousands of years of information that much of the public is only now discovering. Learning about this grand industry is an undertaking for any employee, much less the leader of a business.

Imagine what an entrepreneur would have to go through in a day, balancing studies and business tasks. One cannabis industry owner explained to me that "[Getting into the cannabis industry] was like getting a master's degree, and probably cost me just as much from all of the trials and errors."

Relying on one's strengths won't eliminate the need to learn the industry's past. While newcomers are needed and provide fresh insights, some lack the understanding of the plant. As DeAngelo explained, "The mainstream professionals who come to the cannabis industry often bring a needed skill set, but rarely do they have any significant length of experience with cannabis." This is an issue that DeAngelo expects to loom over the industry for some time. "The complexity of cannabis is not something that you learn in a year or two or even three years. If you really want to understand cannabis, it takes a decade or two of experience in this industry."

With such a predicament, DeAngelo sees this education gap having an effect on the industry for the next few decades. Even so, it does not mean that an entrepreneur has to struggle until they acquire enough information. Instead, it allows an opportunity to connect as the cannabis community has always advocated for.

"For the next ten or twenty years, the only way mainstream business professionals get the benefit of the subject matter is to work with experts," DeAngelo noted. "On the other hand, legacy cannabis folks spent much of our career in the underground or in a grey market." With such diverse backgrounds, DeAngelo is one who sees ample room to connect legacy folks and newcomers for mutually beneficial gains.

If an education gap wasn't enough of an indicator, cannabis entrepreneurs should understand how difficult a new cannabis venture is today. After a professional football career in the NFL, Dr. Hervé Damas, MD, knows a thing or two about hard work—and a cannabis business is just that. Dr. Damas compared launching and running Grassroots Wellness to another. "The so-called green rush is an ultra-endurance marathon, not a sprint."

In an early 2019 article, *Barron's* named seven American companies that could win the American green rush. They included Curaleaf, Harvest Health & Recreation, Green Thumb Industries, Acreage Holdings, MedMen, Trulieve Cannabis, and iAnthus Capital Holdings. Some of the reasons these companies made the list include strategic mergers and acquisitions, which allowed companies like Curaleaf to operate in thirteen different states. Other traits include having the income to burn, but doing so judiciously so that profits are generated. While these traits to success may not be feasible to newcomers, it is best to understand the nature of the market competition. These may become sources of an entrepreneur's exit strategy. Doing so can fund the next investment, and its growth plans like these following companies currently embark on.

In addition to the usual highs and lows of any other industry, cannabis requires plenty of regulatory checks and compliance. For example, an idea may be viable in California but not in Colorado or Oregon, but can be allowed in Washington if it meets specific state regulations. Such regulatory hurdles are why there is such a demand for compliance officers and lawyers to ensure that a business stays on the right side of the law.

The long, grueling task it takes to complete a marathon is spot on for any business venture, but especially in today's cannabis space. One must be aware that this is not a get rich quick scheme; it is for the long haul and the right reasons. If not, an entrepreneur could find themselves out of a significant investment thanks to a lack of knowledge or passion for its product or service. A passion for the plant is required, otherwise one is unlikely to make it through this industry's foundational time.

"This is not for the light of heart," explained Autumn Shelton of Autumn Brands. "There are so many hurdles to go through that it takes real tenacity; the ability to know when to spend money and when not to." Even so, Shelton added that, "Since this industry is so new, there is no ceiling for who can be a leader or a participant."

The pain points of the cannabis industry share the same frustrations as other spaces have. Brett Fink, SVP of cannabis cultivators Old Pal, believes that cannabis does embody numerous pain points other industries can relate to. Much like DeAngelo's vision for success over the next two decades, Fink sees the benefit in learning from skilled leaders in and out of the sector. "We need to learn from past mistakes and bring on folks who know and can operate at a high capacity."

Bringing on the right kind of people helps keep a company away from bad publicity and potential financial or legal devastation. With some of cannabis's top companies creating controversy for themselves that run the misconduct gamut, effective leadership is that much more important to the industry—keeping the company on the right side of the news and law. While top minds won't entirely ensure that a company's public perception remains positive, it often does an effective job of keeping things in check.

Perception also extends to the entrepreneur themselves. While eccentric figures have excelled in other industries, often the classic business leader is the face of the company. That is likely taking shape in cannabis, but not even close to other industries. In this space, eccentric has been the name of the game for years. As such, personality is allowed and welcomed.

For a perfect example, revert back to Steve DeAngelo. By combining a tailored suit with his long braids, gauged ears, and signature hat, he may not look like every Fortune 500 leader. That said, he fits right into the counterculture leaders who now head businesses that may one day be part of the Fortune 500. In short, there is no ideal look for a business leader in cannabis. Strait-laced and tye dye alike are welcome, as long as they remain ethical, produce results, and avoid controversy.

Regarding perception and the success of the business as a whole, there will be always ups and downs. That is a guarantee this industry will not be able to run from (nor has any other). Those ups and downs can be that much more significant in the burgeoning cannabis space. Such amplified highs and lows can stem from numerous reasons, one of the main being the gaps needed for products and services.

With such a demand for more products and services, the cannabis space offers newcomers a rare opportunity: The chance to be seen as a leader in short order. The best products and services are going to win out, so whoever is behind the project is going to reap the benefits. As such, many respondents said that age and background are not a concern in the industry. Instead, merit wins out.

Access to capital and other hurdles do make some believe that background issues can still be revised to improve the industry. Much is required to correct this gap, but some states have begun to ensure that a correction is made. They include Massachusetts, whose Cannabis Control Commission launched a social equity program in the summer of 2018. The program promotes and encourages those from minority communities impacted by the War on Drugs to gain access to licenses and ownership.

While the industry lacks in providing access to people of color and women, most respondents believe that the sector is doing more than other spaces. Brett Gelfand believes that the industry allows for an immense opportunity for young entrants into the marketplace. The young business leader considers building cannabis-related companies "the ultimate experience for me as a young entrepreneur." He went on to elaborate that, "Up-and-coming cannabis companies are staffed by passionate individuals from extremely diverse demographics. The cannabis industry has been the greatest playing field for me as a young entrepreneur since I am learning along with the rest of the industry."

The 2017 Women and Minorities report from *Marijuana Business Daily* found that women-owned businesses made up over a quarter of those it surveyed. It reported that, "Over a quarter of survey respondents who launched a cannabis business and/or have an ownership stake in a marijuana company are women— closely mirroring the percentage of executive positions in the MJ industry occupied by females. Ancillary services firms and ancillary tech and products companies are ahead of the pack when it comes to the percentage of female owners and founders. These companies can get off the ground with relatively little capital and without the need to obtain a license because they don't actually touch the plant."

Not all sectors were alike. With the cannabis industry average of women-owned businesses at 26 percent, ancillary services firms saw 43.3 percent of its businesses owned by women. However, many fell under the average. Infused products and wholesale cultivators were just short of the average, at 25 and 22.2 percent. Meanwhile, vertically integrated businesses and investors made were just 14.6 and 11 percent women owned.

Of those polled, *Marijuana Business Daily* found that 40 percent planned to expand their company into a new market within the next year, just 3 percent lower than male responses. "A sizable majority of female and male leaders who plan to take their companies into new markets have identified opportunities in both the medical and recreational sides of the industry, though a larger percentage of women-led companies are moving into medical-only markets," the report noted.

The state with the most women-owned businesses were California, Colorado, and Oregon—though only California (34.5 percent) and Colorado (32.4 percent) exceeded the cannabis industry average.

More concerning may be the disparity of ownership in the industry. *Marijuana Business Daily's* report found that 81 percent of it respondents were white business owners. Other made up the second largest group at just 6.7 percent. Latinx (5.7 percent), African American (4.3 percent), and Asian (2.4 percent) rounded out the list. While additional diversity ownership endeavors do seem to be in operation in 2019, the chasm remains massive and could grow due to increased mergers and acquisitions.

Numerous cannabis proponents, both legacy and newer

entrants, hope to see the industry shape the market and not vice versa. As such, those that endeavor to advance the cannabis ethos continue to champion the community. Except, this time, instead of smoking grass and talking about life and philosophy, the people are discussing customer demographics and company philosophy...though some are still smoking grass while doing so.

Joyce Cenali of Big Rock Partners used a classic team quote to summarize the current state of the market. "For the most part, the people that make up the companies in this space realize that all ships rise together."

A community doesn't stop at business leaders for many in the cannabis industry. In fact, it doesn't start there either. Instead, it is about the people that benefit from the plant. As Sasha Perelman explained, "That cannabis is a truly magical plant and helps people immensely." She went on to describe her own experience with the community. "Reading story after story about life-changing states of being for people, especially kids, suffering from debilitating conditions and the role cannabis has played in their transformative wellness is incredibly moving. I'm mesmerized by the impact of this plant medicine to mental and emotional well-being that affects hundreds of millions of people. Shouldn't this conversation be much louder?"

While it may seem like the pot game is easy, that is far from the truth. Consider all the successful entrepreneurs who have lost their shirt on out-of-their-strength ventures like opening a restaurant or running a farm. There is a good chance that many hapless entrepreneurs will now attempt to pivot to losing their shirt in cannabis thanks to its booming popularity and need. Don't let it happen to your endeavor.

Launching and growing your own business will always be an arduous journey. Be it a first-timer or veteran, entrepreneurs understand the gravity of their undertaking. While cannabis adds extra hurdles and headaches to the process, the fruits of many companies' labor has already come to the forefront. These successes can be found on the stock market, as well as in countless press releases.

With innovation and legalization both continuing to progress, new opportunities are opening up. Entrepreneurs need to keep an eye out on emerging industries to see where their strengths may be best suited. Once they have determined their business and a hungry audience, the real work sets in. As people like DeAngelo have shown, there is a light at the end of the tunnel that opens up on the lucrative gains the industry offers. With the education, passion, and determination needed, you too could become the next great cannabis entrepreneur.

15

Maintaining Cannabis Culture

Cannabis's rapid growth in America continues to strain its identity and ethics. The growing industry already had its issues surrounding the preservation of cannabis ethos as big business crept into the picture. Thanks to the War on Drugs, a slew of additional pressing topics make maintaining legacy cannabis ethics an essential part of the nascent industry. If it fails to do so, then the once-in-a-lifetime opportunity to start an industry off on an equal, ethical footing dies.

Many in the sector feel that the discussion around diversity and inclusion has already faded from the forefront of many minds as profits and growth continue. This is on display at many mainstream circles where inclusion and diversity are discussed less and less at certain events. That said, others in the industry still champion the need to set an example for other industries.

Through the course of my interviews for this book, a mixed perception of the industry's access to people of color and women came about. Some reported that the industry was open and accessible to all. In this time of the green rush, anyone and everyone can find access and success. This may be true to specific sectors or organizations, but the data shows that it is not the case across the industry. While performing better than industry averages, many demand that cannabis do more for a variety of reasons.

One such group demanding more is The People's Dispensary. It started in Oakland in 2016 to serve the needs of people of color, women, queer people, veterans, and those formerly incarcerated. Its client base quickly grew to 4,000 members. In addition to serving these communities, the dispensary uplifts these communities as well. Its equity structure allows people to bring dispensaries to town while enriching communities.

Christine de la Rosa, a co-founder of The People's Dispensary, told me how her work is rewarding as she is dispensing life-saving medicine. However, the effects of the War on Drugs taints the experience. She highlighted the disproportionate rate of arrests between whites and those of color and the resulting economic disparity and social injustice. "White dudes in ties are out here making hella money while black and brown people do the exact same thing for years are in prison."

This issue extends to states with record expungement regulations in their proposed recreational bills. As Leo Bridgewater mentioned in the policy and government chapter, states considering only small-amount possessions for expungement lack the progressive and corrective steps needed to get people out of prison and back into the market as a legal participant. More so, some states aren't seeking to correct marijuana convictions at all.

If this becomes law, then these states continue to cut people of color out of the industry. There is no corrective action, and people remain locked up for possession of cannabis. Meanwhile, communities aren't able to reap the benefits of the legal market as largely white male ran businesses often fills the void.

Looking at the statistics, the War on Drugs clearly targeted communities of color, shattering lives and families for decades. Data compiled by Mary Magazine from DrugWarFacts.org revealed the impact of the War on Drugs. Some staggering facts include:

- Amount spent annually in the US on the war on drugs: **$50+ billion**
- Number of arrests in 2016 in the US for drug law violations: **1,572,579**
- Number of these arrests that were for possession only: **1,249,025 (84 percent)**
- Number of people arrested for a marijuana law violation in 2016: **653,249**
- Number of those charged with marijuana law violations who were arrested for possession only: **574,641 (89 percent)**
- Proportion of people incarcerated for a drug offense in state prison who are Black or Latino, although these groups use and sell drugs at similar rates as whites: **57 percent**

- Number of students who have lost federal financial aid eligibility because of a drug conviction: **200,000+**
- Number of people killed in Mexico's drug war since 2006: **100,000+**
- Number of people killed in the Philippines in drug war since 2016: **10,000+**

At this time, no one is quite certain where the market will head. While advocates, lawmakers, and businesses push for criminal justice reform, others are treating the industry as the cash cow it is. In those cases, ethics be damned. It is about making money and gaining the largest market share in the industry.

Marijuana Business Daily's 2017 Diversity and Women report acknowledged the sensitive issue race has in cannabis, noting that the perception of minority ownership was slightly incorrect. "Over the course of many conversations with prominent figures in the marijuana industry familiar with the topic of diversity and inclusion, it became clear that the findings of our research ran counter to the widely held perceptions that minorities in general have a minuscule presence in the industry."

Despite a more substantial presence than expected, the report was clear to mention that we are still far from reaching fair representation in the industry. "To be sure, minorities still appear to be vastly underrepresented in leadership roles in the cannabis industry. But it doesn't appear to be the 1%-or-less level some people have thrown around publicly," it stated.

Marijuana Business Daily's results also found that a growing number of the workforce identifies as more than one race. Additionally, 7 percent of respondents listed "other" as their ethnicity, making it the second-largest racial category after white.

The report noted that California had the highest concentration of minority-owned businesses, at around 40 percent. Without those numbers, the results would look bleaker. "Many marijuana businesses with minority owners also are clustered in the Golden State, having a significant impact on the overall percentage for the industry. Take California out of the equation, and the ranks of minorities who founded or have stakes in MJ companies plummets," the report noted.

Colorado may be innovating cannabis law, but its ownership is incredibly white. *Marijuana Business Daily* stated that "Colorado ranks in the bottom half of all fifty states in terms of minority-owned businesses in the larger economy, so the relative lack of diversity in the cannabis industry is partly a function of the state's racial composition." The report also noted how economic connections impact any change while operating under the status quo. "Furthermore, Colorado has the most mature marijuana market in the nation, making it hard for any business without substantial resources to survive in such a competitive environment." These sort of financial barriers are of incredible importance, especially in states like New York where the cost of entry is in the multi-millions.

While leadership is diverse, it was not much more than in other industries. The report found that 17 percent of executive positions in cannabis are held by people of color, slightly higher than the national average of 13 percent. The figure represents how minorities are classified, as well as the rise of mixed families, it notes. The number still should be higher according to those who believe that the legal industry should be more accessible to those who were affected by past drug policy. In some states, progress is underway.

"Advocates of racial diversity in the marijuana industry have made meaningful progress in a number of states to influence policy and provide minorities with more opportunities to occupy decision-making roles in cannabis companies. These types of efforts have become more common of late—especially with newly legalized states, like Arkansas, Ohio, and Pennsylvania, which are still developing their marijuana programs—hopefully setting the table for a more diverse cannabis industry down the road."

Concerning women of color, the cannabis community's leadership was slightly above US business averages as well. Women of color made up 5.3 percent of leadership, with the country average at 4.5 percent. Ancillary services represented the highest total at 10 percent, while investors (3 percent) and vertically integrated businesses (1.3 percent) were at the bottom of the sectors listed.

Women in general face a regression in cannabis leadership. In 2015, *Marijuana Business Daily*'s survey found that 36 percent of cannabis executives were women. By 2017, the number was down to 26.9 percent. The industry still sat almost four points above the national average in 2016. The decline in female leadership has been attributed to the green rush.

The report stated, "An increasing number of senior-level male executives from more traditional companies have begun entering the marijuana industry, attracted by explosive sales growth and declining social stigma surrounding cannabis use. Consequently, the executive structure of businesses in the traditional economy—where males occupy more than 75 percent of senior roles—has begun to seep into the marijuana industry."

Like minorities, cannabis leadership for women was higher than the national average, with the industry averaging 27 percent against the national average of 23 percent. Again, ancillary services firms topped the list at 42 percent while investors (10 percent) and vertically integrated businesses (22.7 percent) were at the bottom of the listed sectors. The one outlier of the group was financial services, where women leadership was down in cannabis compared to the national average.

In all, the report painted a troublesome state of the market's leadership, while still reflecting on its better than average numbers. "Relative to their share of the U.S. workforce, both women and minorities are underrepresented in executive positions—and the disparity is even more acute for women of color. There's an absence of robust data regarding the racial composition of the cannabis industry workforce at large, but it's likely this trend extends to marijuana businesses as well." Though, Summer 2019 findings from the outlet could be an indication of more representation for women in these roles.

The issue extends to employees as well. Brett Fink of Old Pal actively seeks out people of color and other backgrounds to make up his team. He found that this isn't always the case in today's industry. "Lots of white men are coming through to the industry. Not many are focusing on diversity in its candidates."

Yet, he noted that most job recruiters send mostly white male candidates for roles. This is a sentiment others shared as well. Those wanting to be allies sometimes don't seem to know where to turn. Fink noted that one of the major cannabis staffing firms that he worked with had sent out a survey for the number of women in the cannabis industry. While it is a start, it may be concerning to some that one of the more prominent staffing agencies has yet to understand the presence of women in the industry.

In other cases, people aren't active in their searches—this doesn't imply that they are against any type of people. Instead, these organizations often believe that it is an organic approach that fixes the diversity gap in the workforce. As Shanel Lindsay of Ardent mentioned in the chapter on board leaders, organic progress has led us to this point where people remain underrepresented. The problem won't fix itself unless adequate measures are set in place.

To make this a reality, groups and lawmakers continue to push for justice reform, inclusion for work, and access to capital to allow women and people of color to participate in the legal market. The People's Dispensary and de la Rosa are part of this continued effort. They believe in the power of cannabis and its ability to transform communities who've been harmed by the War on Drugs and historical criminalization. Its efforts include establishing a grassroots community focused on growing economic power to uplift communities. The group believes that "Equity is not just about the dollars and cents. It's about making sure the new industry bonanza benefits the communities most affected by the War on Drugs. Beyond the sales tax there are many ways that this industry can rebuild communities if we are included!"

Three policy recommendations highlight their suggested changes. They include expanding access and opportunity for generational wealth for the previously incarcerated, additional pathways to industry prosperity, and institutional integrity.

While numbers don't bode much better for current diverse leadership than other industries, that has not affected the spirits of everyone in the space. As *Marijuana Business Daily* co-founder Cassandra Farrington explained in the chapter on executive leadership, she sees what is happening in cannabis as a harbinger of what's to come in the broader economy. In that scenario, women are accepted as equals and the male-dominated upper executive playing field is not, and won't, be established in the industry.

Yet others believe that more can and should be done to

achieve such an outcome. One of those people is Steve DeAngelo, who thinks that access to capital is one of the most significant roadblocks in the industry. "Communities of color in this country, traditionally have had very, very limited access to capital." DeAngelo expanded on the subject and its most trying adversities. "One of the huge obstacles, and there are many obstacles, that people of color have getting into the cannabis industry is getting startup capital." Without this capital or the established connections, a person is unable to become involved in the market, he explained. "If you don't have existing networks, if you haven't grown up in or gotten an education that really prepares you for engaging with investors and with capital markets, it can be an insurmountable problem."

To address this issue, DeAngelo sees the communal cannabis spirit being the solution. In this case, that includes putting its money where its mouth is. "What I would like to see my industry do is come together and see to it that we create a dedicated investment fund. And that investment fund would fund projects to ensure that some of the communities that traditionally are underrepresented have a shot at this."

DeAngelo's hope for communal funding could show that the industry has embraced cannabis ethos and is taking the correct steps to right some of the injustices that have impacted people of color throughout the years. However, declining leadership and uncertainty around employment in each sector leaves many wondering if cannabis is heading in the right direction. Is cannabis ethos evolving into the mainstream, or is the mainstream evolving cannabis?

Sure, numbers in leadership are slightly above industry standards, but is that enough? Many would say no. Declining female leadership has numerous people wondering if the industry will be comprised of white men with all the money. If so, then what was cannabis legalized for? Part of its legalization was to right these wrongs, but if it ends up looking just about as white and male as the rest, then it may seem like its legalization was merely a cash grab that some had long assumed.

With major cannabis companies like MedMen being ousted from the New York City Medical Cannabis Industry Association over claims of racism and homophobia in the office, one has to wonder where cannabis is headed. Is it following the path of Silicon Valley and the woes coming from a lack of representation in STEM fields? Will women and people of color once again be relegated while the ethics of cannabis wash away as the money comes pouring in?

The hope is that those are just fears and that cannabis is setting a new trend for industries. The uptick in representation gives hope to many that this is the case. However, with generations of social and criminal injustice in this country, others in the cannabis community are far from sure that will be the outcome. As such, many will continue to champion for fair access and criminal justice reform in this once in a lifetime opportunity.

It is our responsibility to make the cannabis industry into the model generations have longed for. The question is, will it come to fruition?

Acknowledgments

I would like to thank numerous people for making this book possible. To my family and friends, thank you for asking how I was doing, offering assistance, and never asking why I looked more and more disheveled as the process went along. I'd also like to thank Skyhorse Publishing for giving me the opportunity to write my first book. I hope this won't be the last time we work together. A particular thanks to Jason Katzman for being such a helpful and clear editor. Thank you for making this such a smooth process.

I'd also like to thank my many sources. Above all else, thank you Lulu Tsui. You put me in touch with so many amazing people. The book would not be what it is without your help and willingness to share your community with me. Thank you as well to Ashley Thane and everyone at KCSA, Eamon Levesque at

N6A, Záne Bader at NisonCo, and several other amazing public relations firms and individuals who introduced me to their communities for this book. I apologize if I omit anyone. You are all amazing.

I'd also like to thank the following people and publications for giving me a better understanding of the cannabis industry's careers:

- Lynette Campbell (Zoomers Employment Services)
- James Yagielo (HempStaff)
- Joyce Cenali (Big Rock)
- Spencer Uniss
- Dr. Hervé Damas, MD (Grassroots Medicine and Wellness)
- Helen Cho (Aloha Green Apoth)
- Harry McIlroy, MD
- Eleanor Kuntz, PhD, CEO (LeafWorks)
- Me Fuimaono-Poe
- Shanel Lindsay (Ardent)
- Brad Bogus (Confident Cannabis)
- Eric Vlosky (PurePressure)
- Bryan Passman, Managing Partner (The GIGG, Hunter + Esquire)
- David Hua (Meadow)
- Craig Zaffe (Your CBD Oils)
- Megan Archer (IESO)
- Catia Lopes Nunes (Etain)
- Helen Cho (Aloha Green)
- Heidi Fikstad (Moss Crossing)
- Vince Ning (Nabis)
- The Insight Partners

- Daniel Witt (Sonoma Lab Works)
- Brett Gelfand (CannaBIZ Collects)
- Zack Taylor (Life Insurance 420)
- Tess Woods (Tess Woods PR)
- Benzinga
- Robert Half
- Vangst
- Mary Magazine
- Leafly
- Kym B (TribeTokes)
- Autumn Shelton (Autumn Brands)
- Cassandra Farrington (*Marijuana Business Daily*)
- Nick Kovacevich (KushCo)
- Andrew Livingston (Vincente Sederberg)
- Leland Radovanovic (Power Plant Strategies)
- Steve Deangelo (Harborside)
- Leo Bridgewater
- Ryan Lepore (PrestoDoctor)
- Brian Barkovitz (ABS Engineer)
- Heidi Minx (MinxLive)
- Jyl Ferris (Independent)
- Cain Castor (Good People)
- Serge Chistov (Honest Marijuana Company)
- Cooper Hollmaier (Visiture)
- Heather Carter (REVEL)
- Lewis Goldberg (KCSA)
- Kris Lenz (MGO|ELLO National Cannabis Alliance)
- Amanda Osorio
- Tara Coomans (PrimoPR)
- Alon Alroy (Bizzabo)
- Ellen Hancock

- Sasha Perelman (Revolver Productions and Mary Talks)
- Jacobi Holland (REVEL)
- Natasha Przedborski (PussyWeed)
- Kathryn Han (Thinking of a Blue Dream)
- Alex Howe (Powerplant Global Strategy)
- Jose Nunez, (CEO and Founder of Yerba Organics)
- Christine de la Rosa (People's Dispensary)
- Brett Fink (Old Pal)
- And the numerous sources unable or not wanting to be identified

Thank you all for your time, information, and flexibility in getting me answers. More so, thank you for allowing me into this community. I hope this book serves as an informative glimpse into your world and the importance of its ethics as it becomes the global marketplace it will one day be.

Hope you enjoy, and that this project puts you on the path to a career in cannabis.